PARANORMAL PHENOMENA

OTHER BOOKS OF RELATED INTEREST

OPPOSING VIEWPOINTS SERIES

America Beyond 2001
America's Future
America's Victims
Constructing a Life Philosophy
Death and Dying
Mental Illness
Religion in America
Science & Religion
Space Exploration
21st Century Earth

PARANORMAL PHENOMENA

David L. Bender, *Publisher*

Bruno Leone, *Executive Editor*

Scott Barbour, *Managing Editor*

Brenda Stalcup, *Senior Editor*

Paul A. Winters, *Book Editor*

OPPOSING
VIEWPOINTS®
SERIES

Greenhaven Press, Inc., San Diego, California

Cover photo: Photodisc

Library of Congress Cataloging-in-Publication Data

Paranormal phenomena : opposing viewpoints / Paul A. Winters, book
    editor.
        p.   cm. — (Opposing viewpoints series)
    Includes bibliographical references and index.
    ISBN 1-56510-558-3 (lib. : alk. paper). —
ISBN 1-56510-557-5 (pbk. : alk. paper)
    1. Parapsychology. 2. Unidentified flying objects. 3. Prophecies.
I. Winters, Paul A., 1965–   . II. Series: Opposing viewpoints series
(Unnumbered)
BF1031.P332 1997
133—dc21   96-49921
                                                                          CIP

Greenhaven Press, Inc., P.O. Box 289009
San Diego, CA 92198-9009

"Congress shall make no law...abridging the freedom of speech, or of the press."

First *Amendment* to the U.S. Constitution

The basic foundation of our democracy is the First Amendment guarantee of freedom of expression. The Opposing Viewpoints Series is dedicated to the concept of this basic freedom and the idea that it is more important to practice it than to enshrine it.

CONTENTS

Chapter 3: Does ESP Exist?

Chapter 4: Does Life After Death Exist?

Why Consider Opposing Viewpoints?

"The only way in which a human being can make some approach to knowing the whole of a subject is by hearing what can be said about it by persons of every variety of opinion and studying all modes in which it can be looked at by every character of mind. No wise man ever acquired his wisdom in any mode but this."

John Stuart Mill

In our media-intensive culture it is not difficult to find differing opinions. Thousands of newspapers and magazines and dozens of radio and television talk shows resound with differing points of view. The difficulty lies in deciding which opinion to agree with and which "experts" seem the most credible. The more inundated we become with differing opinions and claims, the more essential it is to hone critical reading and thinking skills to evaluate these ideas. Opposing Viewpoints books address this problem directly by presenting stimulating debates that can be used to enhance and teach these skills. The varied opinions contained in each book examine many different aspects of a single issue. While examining these conveniently edited opposing views, readers can develop critical thinking skills such as the ability to compare and contrast authors' credibility, facts, argumentation styles, use of persuasive techniques, and other stylistic tools. In short, the Opposing Viewpoints Series is an ideal way to attain the higher-level thinking and reading skills so essential in a culture of diverse and contradictory opinions.

In addition to providing a tool for critical thinking, Opposing Viewpoints books challenge readers to question their own strongly held opinions and assumptions. Most people form their opinions on the basis of upbringing, peer pressure, and personal, cultural, or professional bias. By reading carefully balanced opposing views, readers must directly confront new ideas as well as the opinions of those with whom they disagree. This is not to simplistically argue that everyone who reads opposing views will—or should—change his or her opinion. Instead, the series enhances readers' understanding of their own views by encouraging confrontation with opposing ideas. Careful examination of others' views can lead to the readers' understanding of the logical inconsistencies in their own opinions, perspective on why they hold an opinion, and the consideration of the possibility that their opinion requires further evaluation.

EVALUATING OTHER OPINIONS

To ensure that this type of examination occurs, Opposing Viewpoints books present all types of opinions. Prominent spokespeople on different sides of each issue as well as well-known professionals from many disciplines challenge the reader. An additional goal of the series is to provide a forum for other, less known, or even unpopular viewpoints. The opinion of an ordinary person who has had to make the decision to cut off life support from a terminally ill relative, for example, may be just as valuable and provide just as much insight as a medical ethicist's professional opinion. The editors have two additional purposes in including these less known views. One, the editors encourage readers to respect others' opinions—even when not enhanced by professional credibility. It is only by reading or listening to and objectively evaluating others' ideas that one can determine whether they are worthy of consideration. Two, the inclusion of such viewpoints encourages the important critical thinking skill of objectively evaluating an author's credentials and bias. This evaluation will illuminate an author's reasons for taking a particular stance on an issue and will aid in readers' evaluation of the author's ideas.

As series editors of the Opposing Viewpoints Series, it is our hope that these books will give readers a deeper understanding of the issues debated and an appreciation of the complexity of even seemingly simple issues when good and honest people disagree. This awareness is particularly important in a democratic society such as ours in which people enter into public debate to determine the common good. Those with whom one disagrees should not be regarded as enemies but rather as people whose views deserve careful examination and may shed light on one's own.

Thomas Jefferson once said that "difference of opinion leads to inquiry, and inquiry to truth." Jefferson, a broadly educated man, argued that "if a nation expects to be ignorant and free . . . it expects what never was and never will be." As individuals and as a nation, it is imperative that we consider the opinions of others and examine them with skill and discernment. The Opposing Viewpoints Series is intended to help readers achieve this goal.

David L. Bender & Bruno Leone,
Series Editors

INTRODUCTION

"Open-mindedness [regarding paranormal phenomena] is not an act of intellectual generosity. It is the appropriate response to what we currently know, and don't know."

Stuart Appelle

"We must be fair-minded and objective. But at some point . . . we have to debunk [the paranormal] to keep alive an appreciation for the reflective mind."

Paul Kurtz

In surveys conducted by national polling firms, roughly half of Americans consistently report that they believe in such paranormal phenomena as ghosts, communication with the deceased, reincarnation, extrasensory perception (ESP), and clairvoyance. Eight million people claim to have had a near-death experience. Nineteen million say that they have seen an unidentified flying object (UFO), and four million report that they have been abducted by aliens.

Skeptical scientists reject the existence of such phenomena on the grounds that there is no convincing scientific proof. They decry belief in the paranormal as an example of antiscientific attitudes that promote disdain for the principles of science and reason. However, parapsychologists and others who use scientific methods to explore unexplained phenomena contend that there is overwhelming anecdotal evidence to suggest that many of these phenomena are real. They maintain that rejecting the possibility of the existence of the paranormal without exploration is itself unscientific.

Controversial reports from people claiming to have been abducted and subjected to biological experiments by aliens illustrate the debate between parapsychologists and skeptics. Like many parapsychologists, John E. Mack, a Harvard psychiatrist and the author of *Abductions: Human Encounters with Aliens*, believes that the alien abduction phenomenon can be explored with scientific techniques. Mack has interviewed and psychoanalyzed dozens of people who claim to have been abducted by aliens, and he has used hypnotic regression to uncover their abduction memories. He argues that there is both anecdotal and physical evidence to support the hypothesis that the phenomenon is real.

Mack contends that the abduction accounts, reported by individuals who have no apparent reason for deception, are remarkably consistent, which suggests they are more than fabrications or fantasies. In Mack's opinion, the abductees he interviewed "were very straightforward, healthy-minded folks who had had these unusual experiences." The encounters they relate follow a fairly uniform pattern. The abductee awakens in a state of paralysis with a feeling that there is an alien presence in the room. Unable to resist, he or she is floated from the bedroom and taken to an awaiting spaceship. The experiencer is subjected to a biological examination in which samples of hair, skin, sperm or ova, and other tissues are taken and a tracking device is implanted. Finally, he or she is returned to his or her room with all conscious memories of the experience erased (only later to be recovered). From his psychiatric evaluation of a substantial number of experiencers, Mack concluded that "their stories jibed . . . and it all seemed very real."

To further support his contention that the alien abduction phenomenon is genuine, Mack points to physical evidence such as signs of psychological trauma among experiencers, scars on abduction victims, and "implants" (foreign objects removed from abductees' bodies). He argues that the trauma exhibited by abductees is not the result of psychosis or fantasy and therefore must have a basis in real experience. Psychiatric tests performed by independent researchers confirm that abductees are otherwise mentally healthy individuals, which Mack cites in support of his hypothesis. Of the implants, he contends that microscopic and electrochemical tests have failed to identify them as being of earthly origin, leaving open the possibility that they are extraterrestrial. "In virtually every case," Mack asserts, "there are one or more concrete physical findings that accompany or follow the abduction experience."

Skeptics retort, however, that there is no conclusive evidence to support claims of alien abduction. They contend that it is extremely unlikely that life on other planets exists—let alone intelligent life capable of interstellar travel. Therefore, they argue, consideration of otherworldly kidnappers as the explanation for alien abduction reports is beyond the pale of science and reason.

Renowned skeptic Susan Blackmore, a senior lecturer in psychology at the University of the West of England, has attempted to debunk the alien abduction reports. She argues that there is a simpler and more plausible explanation for the experiences of so-called abductees. Research by psychologists Nicholas P. Spanos, Patricia A. Cross, Kirby Dickson, and Susan C. DuBreuil has shown that many abductees suffer from a sleep disorder known as sleep paralysis, she points out. According to Blackmore, normal sleep brings on a harmless paralysis of muscles that prevents people from acting out their dreams. About one in five persons has experienced waking from sleep while this paralysis persists, she maintains. Such sleep paralysis, she asserts, is often accompanied by hypnagogic hallucinations or by a related sleep disturbance called false awakening, in which people dream that they have awakened but in fact are still dreaming.

Blackmore and other skeptics note that many different cultures past and present have built elaborate myths around sleep paralysis. In past times, tales of the incubus and succubus—demons who stole the chastity of unwilling sleeping victims—were common, according to Blackmore. With prevailing cultural myths about UFOs and extraterrestrials, she contends, it is no wonder that people today dream about being abducted by aliens. Vivid hallucinations related to sleep disturbances could explain the psychological trauma noted in those who report alien abductions, Blackmore maintains. Abductees' physical scars could have entirely mundane causes, she argues, and there is no evidence that the "implants" recovered from these people's bodies are of extraterrestrial origin. In the absence of extraordinary evidence to support claims of extraterrestrial kidnappings, Blackmore asserts, hallucinations related to sleep disorders should be accepted as the most likely explanation of the phenomenon.

Skeptics maintain that extraordinary claims involving paranormal phenomena such as UFOs and alien abductions require extraordinary evidence. Without scientific proof of the existence of the paranormal, they argue, these phenomena should be considered hallucinations or superstitions. Parapsychologists, however, contend that paranormal phenomena should be studied with scientific methods and that to reject the supernatural out-of-hand is itself unscientific. The ongoing debate between parapsychologists and skeptics over the existence of the paranormal is presented in the following chapters: Is Belief in Paranormal Phenomena Unscientific? Are UFOs Extraterrestrial Spacecraft? Does ESP Exist? Does Life After Death Exist?

CHAPTER 1

Is Belief in Paranormal Phenomena Unscientific?

CHAPTER PREFACE

The commercial success of a few shows dramatizing investigations of the paranormal, such as The X-Files and Sightings, has led to the creation of a number of other television shows featuring UFOs, alien abductions, government conspiracies, psychics, and angels. At the same time, according to surveys by Gallup, CNN, and USA Today, over 70 percent of Americans say they believe in miracles and angels, 50 percent believe in UFOs, and nearly 25 percent believe in reincarnation, life after death, and astrology. Skeptics and enthusiasts of the paranormal dispute whether these shows contribute to Americans' belief in the supernatural.

Glenn Sparks, an associate professor of communications at Purdue University in West Lafayette, Indiana, has conducted surveys to measure the relationship between watching such programs and belief in the paranormal. He argues that viewers of these shows are less capable than others of thinking critically about both paranormal events and real phenomena. The Committee for Scientific Investigation of Claims of the Paranormal (CSICOP), a group of skeptical scientists, decries the influence of television in promoting what they call unscientific beliefs. "A lot of people believe this [material] because it's on television," maintains Paul Kurtz, chairman of CSICOP.

Aficionados of the paranormal maintain that rather than promoting superstition, such shows merely provide entertainment. Chris Carter, creator and producer of The X-Files, maintains that the stories for his show are drawn from already existing beliefs in the paranormal. But, he asserts, "It's fiction . . . we make this stuff up." Mack Anderson, producer of The Paranormal Borderline, a news magazine show featuring tales of the paranormal, argues that society's openness to the paranormal has fueled the development of these programs. The stories presented on the programs are made believable, he contends, by the credibility of the witnesses.

While some scientists express concern that the portrayal of paranormal phenomena on television contributes to an antiscientific attitude among viewers, those who produce and watch the programs argue that the shows simply draw on material from popular culture. The viewpoints in the following chapter debate whether belief in the existence of paranormal phenomena is unscientific.

| "The scientific method must be employed as the basis for drawing conclusions regarding paranormal claims."

BELIEF IN PARANORMAL PHENOMENA IS UNSCIENTIFIC

Bryan Farha

In the following viewpoint, Bryan Farha presents an exercise in logical thinking and argues that many people jump to illogical conclusions when confronted with mysterious phenomena, assuming that just because an explanation is possible, it is likely. Because the existence of paranormal phenomena is unlikely, he contends, claims of the paranormal should be subjected to scientific scrutiny. Farha is chair of the department of Behavioral Studies and Counseling Psychology at Oklahoma City University.

As you read, consider the following questions:

1. According to Farha, what two questions must be asked in investigating the "phantom" newspaper?
2. In the author's opinion, what conclusion do many people jump to regarding UFOs?

From Bryan Farha, "Looking Up to Logic," *Skeptical Inquirer*, January/February 1996. Reprinted by permission of the Committee for the Scientific Investigation of Claims of the Paranormal.

I magine you live in the small City of Salina, Kansas. As is typical of Kansas weather, it is a fairly windy morning. There is
much debris blowing in your front yard, including leaves,
branches, and twigs; the children's toys; and garbage resulting
from the trash container having been blown over.

On the lawn of your residence, about twenty feet from your
doorstep, you see what looks like a newspaper amongst all the
debris. Because of the adverse conditions, it is somewhat difficult to clearly see the print on the paper. But you do not subscribe
to the local newspaper. Upon further inspection, and to your absolute bewilderment, you seem to be able to make out the
words "London Times" at the top. Also on page one, there appears
to be a large photograph of the football team that won the Super
Bowl the previous day. The images are a bit fuzzy, but it certainly
seems as though the London Times is headlining the previous day's
Super Bowl, which is not unusual for any paper. It seems rather
bizarre, however, that an apparently current newspaper from another country would find its way to your lawn in Salina, Kansas.
You do not, nor have you ever, subscribed to the London Times.
Your curiosity and interest are escalating. So you go to your bedroom to put on a robe and slippers and then go outside in order
to get a much closer look to determine if your eyes are deceiv-
ing you. But now, the "phantom" paper is gone. You check your
neighbors' yards, but no paper is in sight.

POSSIBLE EXPLANATIONS FOR THE "PHANTOM NEWSPAPER"

How can this experience be explained? There are several possibilities. But the question must be addressed from two perspectives: (1) Was the perception, in fact, what the observer thought
it was? (2) If the argument is plausible, under what conditions
could it be accounted for?

Concerning the first perception, there are myriad factors to
consider. Recalling the wind and resulting debris, was this actually a newspaper or could it have been wrapping paper, someone else's trash, or even reflected sunlight? If, in fact, it was a
newspaper, can we verify that it was the London Times? That it was a
photograph of the recent Super Bowl champions on the front
page? What tangible evidence exists of your experience?

Concerning the second perception, how does a current issue
of the London Times find its way to your residential lawn in Salina,
Kansas? It is possible that the newspaper belonged to a neighbor
and the wind blew it into your yard; this notion is easily supported or refuted with a small degree of legwork. But if this legwork does not yield a satisfactory explanation, we might then

ask a series of other questions. If this, too, fails to provide adequate explanation, we then become faced with very tenuous possibilities. One such possibility is that a newspaper carrier from London, England, came to Salina, Kansas, by plane and delivered the paper to your house. Remote as this seems, it is a possibility. Not a perfectly logical or feasible answer, but the possibility is there.

Likely vs. Unlikely Assumptions

A while back I received a typed letter from America that the writer had dated the nineteenth of the month. Nothing remarkable in this, except that I received it on the fifteenth of the month. Now, this could be a case of superluminal velocity of mail delivery. It could also be a case where the writer hit the nine key when he or she meant to hit the zero; and as the envelope was postmarked the tenth of the month, I was, and still am, more inclined to opt for the latter explanation. You see how otherwise miraculous or inexplicable facts are explained by careful, logical deduction of which any rational person might be proud. What it all really boils down to is: What is the least unlikely assumption that can possibly be made in accordance with the known facts?

Ralph Estling, *Skeptical Inquirer*, May/June 1996.

It is at this point that drawing plausible conclusions based on logic becomes critical. Unfortunately, it is also at this point that much of the general public errs in drawing conclusions based on available evidence. A case in point: An object in the night sky is unidentified. This *does* make the object a UFO. But the term "UFO" only means that the object cannot be identified. If evidence is insufficient to ascertain its identity (or its reality), then the conclusions we can draw are very limited. Why, then, do so many jump to the conclusion that if *we can't identify the object, then it must be an alien spacecraft from another solar system or galaxy?* Understand, it might be an alien spacecraft, but before we can draw this conclusion we must have *substantial* evidence. Assuming that an unidentified object in the sky is an alien spacecraft is as tenuous and potentially erroneous as attributing the arrival of the English newspaper to Salina, Kansas, via a London carrier traveling by airplane. Yet in the newspaper example, we easily recognize the faulty thinking involved in making the assumption (hypostatic leap) of a Londoner making an unexplained home delivery to a nonsubscribing Kansas resident.

PARANORMAL BELIEVERS SEEM TO ABANDON LOGIC

Why, then, does the UFO phenomenon seem to change the thinking process of so many? Is the UFO phenomenon, as well as other potentially anomalistic (paranormal) experiences, so intriguing that people allow it to alter their understanding of logical thinking? It is possible that alien spacecraft visit Earth, that abductions occur, that evangelists can reverse disease, that objects can move without apparent impetus, and that "ghosts" exist. But a word of caution: We cannot make positive conclusions about these phenomena without evidence, substantiation, and the use of logic. In other words, the scientific method must be employed as the basis for drawing conclusions regarding paranormal claims. Science is not a panacea for all explanation, but regarding paranormal claims it remains, by far, the best method. Let's not fall into the trap of abandoning science and logic because of curiosity and imagination. Rather, let's use curiosity and imagination as a springboard to the scientific method in order to draw accurate conclusions regarding mysteries of the universe.

| "[Scientists'] rejection [of ghosts is] not exactly based on the method of science or even its spirit."

AN OPEN MIND ABOUT PARANORMAL PHENOMENA IS SCIENTIFIC

Roger L. Welsch

In the following viewpoint, Roger L. Welsch describes an experiment probing what he calls the folk beliefs of scientists. He contends that because many scientists automatically reject the possibility that ghosts exist, they fail to exercise the scientific method. Science requires an objective investigation into unexplained phenomena such as ghosts, he argues. Welsch, a folklorist and a former professor of folklore studies, is the author of *Touching the Fire: Buffalo Dancers, the Sky Bundle, and Other Tales.*

As you read, consider the following questions:

1. According to Welsch, why do folklorists use the term *belief* rather than *superstition*?
2. What are the two errors that his student made concerning science, according to the author?
3. In the author's opinion, what rational, agnostic position should scientists take toward the existence of ghosts?

Reprinted from Roger L. Welsch, "A Spirited Disagreement," with permission from *Natural History* magazine (December 1995).

The popular meaning of the word *folklore*—faulty thinking, silly superstition, baseless tradition—is not the way we folklorists use it in our studies. As (ahem) academicians, scholars, scientists, we try to be more objective about the belief systems of others. So, folklorists label traditionally held ideas *beliefs* rather than *superstitions*. There is, after all, some reason to suspect there is accumulated wisdom, even empirical knowledge, in a lot of those venerable belief systems.

Take belief in ghosts, for example, a phenomenon common to a lot of people and a lot of cultures over a lot of time. (If you think I'm stretching the notion, David Hufford goes even further in his introduction to Michiko Iwasaka and Barre Toelken's *Ghosts and the Japanese*: "Ghosts [are] a concept found in all cultures and at all times of which we have any record.") One of the reasons I consider folklore studies a paragon of the sciences is that folklorists consider such things as ghosts.

A SURVEY OF SCIENTISTS' BELIEFS

Back when I was teaching, I had my second-year folklore students do limited fieldwork projects, if at all possible within their own cultural milieus, or subcultures. One young man came to my office after I gave that assignment in class, baffled about where to turn. He told me he was studying science, loved science, believed in science, trusted science, and couldn't imagine that there would be much in the way of folklore he might find in science. "Scientists don't have superstitions," he insisted.

This young man posed a special problem—and opportunity—for me. He was a nice enough guy, but he had succumbed to the arrogance of "omni-science": not just the minor error of thinking science can know all but also the maxigoof of believing science already knows all. How could I make him realize that every area of human experience or endeavor, including technology and science, has its traditions?

"How about working with a traditionally held belief within the scientific community?" I asked him. "Perhaps an idea members of the scientific faculty have that is without obvious scientific basis—something based on personal, emotional inclination rather than empirical knowledge."

"Sounds like superstition to me," he said suspiciously.

"Well, yes, except we don't call. . . .

"I know, I've heard you say it in class a dozen times: 'the word *superstition* is a pejorative, so we folklorists use the term *belief* instead.'"

"So then, how about something like ghosts?"

He snorted in disbelief. "Not a single person in that entire science building believes there are ghosts. Do you believe there are ghosts, Professor Welsch?"

"I don't know."

"Have you ever seen one?"

"I may have but I'm not sure. But you don't have to go into that for this assignment. Just find out if your scientist friends believe there might be such things as ghosts, nothing more or less."

PARANORMAL TOPICS SHOULD NOT BE DISMISSED

Proclaiming that some subjects are not worth studying undermines the checks and balances of science. I have less trust in UFOlogy than in particle physics, not because UFOlogists are necessarily unscientific, but because the social injunction against studying UFOs means there is less of the to-and-fro essential to critical analysis of research.

So let us hear what UFOlogists have to say. Of course, their hypotheses are, like those of all scientists, guilty until proven innocent. If we decide, personally, that UFOs are not worth our while, then we must be clear that is a statement about us, not about UFOs.

George Musser, *Mercury*, January/February 1995.

And that's what the student did. He returned to my office a few weeks later, triumphant. "I told you," he said, handing me his report. "Not a single person in that huge building, in any department, believes there are such things as ghosts. Superstition has no home in science."

"I wonder," I said, pointing out that in this country if you round up a couple of eyewitnesses, you can send someone to death row, and yet there are tens of thousands, hundreds of thousands who not only believe there are such things as ghosts but believe they have seen them. All around the world, in culture after culture, people believe there are ghosts and that they are seen, sometimes on a regular basis. How many eyewitnesses would we have to have, I wondered aloud, before science would assume the rational, agnostic position that there is plenty of evidence something is going on, but that we don't know what it is?

THE METHOD OF SCIENCE VS. SUPERSTITION

Obviously, scientific truth is not a matter of taking a popular vote, and there is the problem of proving a negative, but my student friend had to admit it was curious how quickly and strongly his faculty had rejected the *idea* of ghosts. And he amazed himself when he came to the conclusion, on his own, that this rejection was not exactly based on the method of science or even its spirit. In fact, he said, wringing his hands and screwing up his brow in mock pain, "It's almost like . . . like . . . superstition!" He spit the word out like an epithet. Or an admission.

"Yes, it is," I said, trying to comfort the lad. "But let's give scientists the benefit of the doubt or at least the courtesy an ethnographer would extend to any resource in any fieldwork problem. They may, after all, be right in their rejection of ghosts. There may be nothing at all but our imaginations at work. Or some other natural phenomenon that we do not yet understand. So, let's not call it superstition, okay?"

"Yeah, I know," he said with resignation. "Belief. Scientists have . . . (gasp, choke) . . . folk beliefs."

"And having conducted this survey, do you now believe there are such things as ghosts?" I asked.

He got his A for the project because he answered without hesitation, "I don't know; I'm a scientist, after all."

| "The huge increase in paranormal beliefs is symptomatic of a profound antiscience attitude."

BELIEF IN PARANORMAL PHENOMENA IS ANTISCIENTIFIC

Paul Kurtz

Paul Kurtz, professor emeritus of philosophy at the State University of New York at Buffalo, is the founding chairman of the Committee for the Scientific Investigation of Claims of the Paranormal (CSICOP), an organization of skeptics. In the following viewpoint, Kurtz argues that since the 1970s, Americans have lost respect for scientists and have come to believe that science is harmful to society. He maintains that education in rationalism and in the scientific method is needed to counter this antiscientific trend, which he says has been fostered by environmentalists, multiculturalists, believers in paranormal phenomena, and others.

As you read, consider the following questions:
1. In Kurtz's opinion, what are the most vitriolic attacks on science based on?
2. According to the author, what fears have been promoted by those who oppose biogenetic engineering?
3. What is the view of science promoted by multiculturalists, according to Kurtz?

From Paul Kurtz, "The Growth of Antiscience," *Skeptical Inquirer*, Spring 1994. Reprinted by permission of the Committee for the Scientific Investigation of Claims of the Paranormal.

It is paradoxical that today, when the sciences are advancing by leaps and bounds and when the earth is being transformed by scientific discoveries and technological applications, a strong antiscience counterculture has emerged. This contrasts markedly with attitudes toward science that existed in the nineteenth and the first half of the twentieth centuries. Albert Einstein perhaps best typified the high point of the public appreciation of scientists that prevailed at that time. Paul De Kruif (1926), in his book, *The Microbe Hunters*, described the dramatic results that scientists could now achieve in ameliorating pain and suffering and improving the human condition. John Dewey, perhaps the most influential American philosopher in the first half of this century, pointed out the great pragmatic benefits to humankind from the application of scientific methods of thinking to all aspects of human life. But today the mood has radically changed.

A DECLINE IN THE REPUTATION OF SCIENCE

An April 1993 essay by Dennis Overbye in *Time* magazine begins with the following ominous note:

> Scientists, it seems, are becoming the new villains of Western society. . . . We read about them in newspapers faking and stealing data, and we see them in front of congressional committees defending billion-dollar research budgets. We hear them in sound bites trampling our sensibilities by comparing the Big Bang or some subatomic particle to God.

A July 1993 editorial by Richard S. Nicholson in *Science* magazine, referring to the *Time* essay, comments:

> Does this reflect a growing antiscience attitude? If so, the new movie *Jurassic Park* is not going to help. According to both the writer and producer, the movie intentionally has antiscience undertones. Press accounts say that producer Steven Spielberg believes science is "intrusive" and "dangerous."
>
> It is not only outsiders who are being critical. In recent speeches and publications, George Brown, chairman of the House Space, Science and Technology Committee, has seemed to question the very value of science. Brown has observed that despite our lead in science and technology, we still have many societal ills such as environmental degradation and unaffordable health care. Science, he says, has "promised more than it can deliver." Freeman Dyson seems to share some of this view. In a recent Princeton speech, he states, "I will not be surprised if attacks against science become more bitter and more widespread in the next few years, so long as the economic inequities in our society remain sharp and science continues to be predominantly engaged in building toys for the rich."

"Are these just isolated events, or is something more going on?" asks Richard S. Nicholson in the editorial quoted above.

A further sign that science has lost considerable prestige is the 1993 rejection of the superconducting supercollider project by the U.S. Congress. Although the chief reason given was the need to cut the national deficit, one cannot help but feel that this decision reflects the diminishing level of public confidence in scientific research. . . .

THE SCIENTIFIC APPROACH AND THE PARANORMAL

The scientific approach, which has had such powerful effectiveness in extending the frontiers of knowledge, is now under heavy attack. Of special concern has been the dramatic growth of the occult, the paranormal, and pseudosciences, and particularly the promotion of the irrational and sensational in these areas by the mass media. We allegedly have been living in the New Age. Side by side with astronomy there has been a return to astrology, and concomitant with psychology there was the growth of psychical research and parapsychology. The paranormal imagination soars; science fiction has no bounds. This is the age of space travel, and it includes abductions by extraterrestrial beings and unidentified flying objects from other worlds. The emergence of a paranormal worldview competes with the scientific worldview. Instead of tested causal explanations, the pseudosciences provide alternative explanations that compete in the public mind with genuine science. The huge increase in paranormal beliefs is symptomatic of a profound antiscience attitude, which has not emerged in isolation but is part of a wider spectrum of attitudes and beliefs. . . .

CURRENT CHALLENGES TO THE BENEFITS OF SCIENCE

The most vitriolic attacks on science in recent decades have questioned its benefits to society. To a significant extent these criticisms are based on ethical considerations, for they question the value of scientific research and the scientific outlook to humankind. Here are 10 categories of such objections. There are no doubt others.

1. After World War II great anxiety arose about a possible nuclear holocaust. This fear is not without foundation; for there is some danger of fallout from nuclear accidents and testing in the atmosphere, and there is the threat that political or military leaders might embark, consciously or accidentally, upon a devastating nuclear war. Fortunately, for the moment the danger of a thermonuclear holocaust has abated, though it surely has not

disappeared. However, such critiques generated the fear of scientific research, and even, in some quarters, the view that physicists were diabolical beings who, in tinkering with the secrets of nature, held within their grasp the power to destroy all forms of life on this planet. The fear of nuclear radiation also applies to nuclear power plants. The accident at Chernobyl magnified the apprehension of large sectors of the world's population that nuclear energy is dangerous and that nuclear power plants should be closed down. In countries like the United States, no nuclear power plants are being built, although France and many other countries continue to construct them. The nuclear age has thus provoked an antinuclear reaction, and the beneficent symbol of the scientist of the past, Albert Einstein, has to some been transmogrified into a Dr. Strangelove. Although some of the apprehensions about nuclear radiation are no doubt warranted, to abandon nuclear fuel entirely, while the burning of fossil fuels pollutes the atmosphere, leaves few alternatives for satisfying the energy needs of the world. This does not deny the need to find renewable resources, such as solar and wind power, but will these be sufficient?

SCIENCE VS. PSEUDOSCIENCE

I hold there's a kind of Gresham's Law that applies in the confrontation of science and pseudoscience: In the popular imagination, at least, the bad science drives out the good. What I mean is this: If you are awash in lost continents and channeling and UFOs and all the long litany of claims so well exposed in the *Skeptical Inquirer*, you may not have intellectual room for the findings of science. You're sated with wonder.

Carl Sagan, *Skeptical Inquirer*, January/February 1995.

ENVIRONMENTAL PHOBIAS

2. The fear of science can also be traced to some excesses of the environmental movement. Although the environmentalists' emphasis on ecological preservation is a valid concern, it has led at times to the fear that human technology has irreparably destroyed the ozone layer and that the greenhouse effect will lead to the degradation of the entire planet. Such fears often lead to hysteria about all technologies.

3. In large sectors of the population, there is a phobia about any kind of chemical additive. From the 1930s to the 1950s, it was widely held that "better things and better living can be

achieved through chemistry" and that chemicals would improve the human condition. Today there is, on the contrary, a widespread toxic terror—of PCBs and DDT, plastics and fertilizers, indeed of *any* kind of additive—and there is a worldwide movement calling for a return to nature, to organic foods and natural methods. No doubt we need to be cautious about untested chemical additives that may poison the ecosystem, but we should not forget that the skilled use of fertilizers led to the green revolution and a dramatic increase in food production that reduced famine and poverty worldwide.

4. Suspicion of biogenetic engineering is another dimension of the growth of antiscience. From its very inception biogenetic research has met opposition. Many feared that scientists would unleash a new, virulent strain of E. *coli* bacteria into sewer pipes—and then throughout the ecosystem—that would kill large numbers of people. Jeremy Rifkin and others have demanded that all forms of biogenetic engineering research be banned because of its "dehumanizing" effect. A good illustration of this can be seen in the film *Jurassic Park*, produced by Steven Spielberg. Here not only does a Dr. Frankenstein seek to bring back the dead, but we are warned that a new diabolical scientist, in cloning dinosaurs, will unleash ominous forces across the planet. Although there may be some dangers in biogenetic engineering, it offers tremendous potential benefit for humankind—for the cure of genetic diseases as well as the creation of new products. Witness, for example, the production of synthetic insulin.

ATTACKS ON MEDICINE

5. Another illustration of the growth of antiscience is the widespread attack on orthodox medicine. Some of these criticisms have some merit. With the advances of the scientific revolution and the growth of medical technology, we have been able to extend human life, yet many people are kept alive against their will and suffer excruciating pain; and the right to die has emerged as a basic ethical concern. Medical ethicists have correctly pointed out that the rights of patients have often been ignored by the medical and legal professions. In the past physicians were considered authoritarian figures, whose wisdom and skills were unquestioned. But to many vociferous critics today, doctors are demons rather than saviors. The widespread revolt against animal research is symptomatic of the attack on science. Granted that animals should not be abused or made to suffer unnecessary pain, but some animal rights advocates would ban

all medical research on animals.

6. Another illustration of antiscience is the growing opposition to psychiatry. Thomas Szasz has no doubt played a key role here. As a result of his works, large numbers of mental patients were deinstitutionalized. *One Flew Over the Cuckoo's Nest,* by Ken Kesey dramatizes the view that it is often the psychiatrist himself who is disturbed rather than the patient. Many, like Szasz, even deny that there are mental illnesses, though there seems to be considerable evidence that some patients do suffer behavioral disorders and exhibit symptoms that can be alleviated by antipsychotic drugs.

7. Concomitant with the undermining of public confidence in the practice of medicine and psychiatry has been the phenomenal growth in "alternative health cures," from faith healing and Christian Science to the relaxation response, iridology, homeopathy, and herbal medicines. This is paradoxical, because medical science has made heroic progress in the conquering of disease and the development of antibiotics and the highly successful techniques of surgical intervention. These have all been a boon to human health. But now the very viability of medical science itself has been questioned.

ASIAN MYSTICISM VS. SCIENCE

8. Another area of concern is the impact of Asian mysticism, particularly since World War II, whereby Yoga meditation, Chinese Qigong, gurus, and spiritualists have come into the Western world arguing that these ancient forms of knowledge and therapy can lead to spiritual growth and health in a way that modern medicine does not. Unfortunately, there are very few reliable clinical tests of these so-called spiritual cures. What we have are largely anecdotal accounts, but they hardly serve as objective tests of alternative therapies.

9. Another form of antiscience is the revival of fundamentalist religion even within advanced scientific and educational societies. Fundamentalists question the very foundation of scientific culture. Indeed, in the modern world, it is religion, not science, that seems to have emerged as the hope of humankind. Far more money is being poured into religion than into scientific research and education. Especially symptomatic is the continued growth of "scientific creationism" and widespread political opposition to the teaching of evolution in the schools, particularly in the United States.

10. A final area of antiscience is the growth of multicultural and feminist critiques of science education, particularly in the

universities and colleges. The multiculturist view is that science is not universal or transcultural, but relative to the culture in which it emerges. There are, we are told, non-Western and primitive cultures that are as "true" and "valid" as the scientific culture of the Western world. This movement supports the complete relativization of scientific knowledge. The radical feminist indictment of "masculine bias" in science maintains that science has been the expression of "dead, white Anglo-Saxon males"—from Newton to Faraday, from Laplace to Heisenberg. What we must do, the extremists of these movements advise, is liberate humanity from cultural, racist, and sexist expressions of knowledge, and this means scientific objectivity as well. The positive contribution of these movements, of course, is that they seek to open science to more women and minorities. The negative dimension is that multiculturalist demands on education tend to weaken an understanding of the rigorous intellectual standards essential for effective scientific inquiry. Clearly we need to appreciate the scientific contribution of many cultures and the role of women in science throughout history; on the other hand, some multicultural critics undermine the very possibility of objective science.

A NEED FOR SCIENCE EDUCATION

What I have presented is a kaleidoscope illustration of many current trends that are undermining and threaten the future growth of science. They raise many questions. Why has this occurred? How shall those who believe in the value of scientific methods and the scientific outlook respond?

This is a complex problem, and I can only suggest some possible solutions. But unless the scientific community and those connected with it are willing to take the challenge to science seriously, then I fear that the tide of antiscience may continue to rise. Scientific research surely will not be rejected where there are obvious technological uses to be derived from it, at least insofar as economic, political, and military institutions find these profitable. But the decline in the appreciation of the methods of science and in the scientific outlook can only have deleterious effects upon the long-term role of science in civilization.

One reason for the growth of antiscience is a basic failure to educate the public about the nature of science itself. Of crucial significance is the need for public education in the aims of science. We need to develop an appreciation of the general methods of scientific inquiry, its relationship to skepticism and critical thinking, and its demand for evidence and reason in testing claims to truth. The most difficult task we face is to develop an awareness that the methods of science should not only be used in the narrow domains of the specialized sciences, but should also be generalized, as far as possible, to other fields of human interest.

We also need to develop an appreciation for the cosmic outlook of science. Using the techniques of scientific inquiry, scientists have developed theories and generalizations about the universe and the human species. These theories often conflict with theological viewpoints that for the most part go unchallenged. They also often run counter to mystical, romantic, and aesthetic attitudes. Thus it is time for more scientists and interpreters of science to come forward to explain what science tells us about the universe: for example, they should demonstrate the evidence for evolution and point out that creationism does not account for the fossil record; that the evidence points to a biological basis for the mind and that there is no evidence for reincarnation or immortality. Until the scientific community is willing to explicate openly and defend what science tells us about life and the universe, then I fear it will continue to be undermined by the vast ignorance of those who oppose it.

In this process of education, what is crucial is the development of scientific literacy in the schools and in the communications media. Recent polls have indicated that a very small percentage of the U.S. population has any understanding of scientific principles. The figures are similar for Britain, France, and Germany, where large sectors of the population are abysmally unaware of the nature of the scientific outlook. Thus we need to educate the public about how science works and what it tells us about the world, and we should make sure this understanding is applied to all fields of human knowledge.

A NEED FOR SKEPTICISM IN ALL FIELDS

The growth of specialization has made this task enormously difficult. Specialization has enabled people to focus on one field, to pour their creative talents into solving specific problems, whether in biology or physics, mathematics or economics. But we need to develop generalists as well as specialists. Much of the fear and opposition to science is due to a failure to understand the nature of scientific inquiry. This understanding should include an appreciation for what we know and do not know. This means not only an appreciation of the body of reliable knowledge we now possess, but also an appreciation of the skeptical outlook and attitude. The interpreters of science must go beyond specialization to the general explication of what science tells us about the universe and our place in it. This is unsettling to many within society. In one sense, science is the most radical force in the modern world, because scientists need to be prepared to question everything and to demand verification or validation of any claims.

The broader public welcomes scientific innovation. Every new gadget or product and every new application in technology, where it is positive, is appreciated for its economic and social value. What is not appreciated is the nature of the scientific enterprise itself and the need to extend the critical methods of science further, especially to ethics, politics, and religion. Until those in the scientific community have sufficient courage to extend the methods of science and reason as far as they can to these other fields, then I feel that the growth of antiscience will continue.

Now it is not simply the task of scientists who work in the laboratory, who have a social responsibility to the greater society; it is also the task of philosophers, journalists, and those within the corporate and the political world who appreciate the contribution of science to humankind. For what is at stake in a sense is modernism itself. Unless corporate executives and those who wield political power recognize the central role that science and technology have played in the past four centuries, and can continue to play in the future, and unless science is defended, then I fear that the irrational growth of antiscience may undermine the viability of scientific research and the contributions of science in the future. The key is education—education within the schools, but education also within the media. We need to raise the level of appreciation, not simply among students, from grammar school through the university, but among those who control the mass media, and here, alas, the scientific outlook is often overwhelmed by violence, lurid sex, the paranormal, and religious bias.

The world today is a battlefield of ideas. In this context the partisans of science need to defend courageously the authentic role that science has played and can continue to play in human civilization. The growth of antiscience must be countered by a concomitant growth in advocacy of the virtues of science. Scientists are surely not infallible; they make mistakes. But the invaluable contributions of science need to be reiterated. We need public re-enchantment with the ideals expressed by the scientific outlook.

> "There now exists something of a no-man's-land between organized science on the one hand and the public and news media on the other hand, an area that contains topics such as parapsychology."

STUDY OF PARANORMAL PHENOMENA IS NOT ANTISCIENTIFIC

Peter A. Sturrock

The study of anomalies within science and outside of mainstream science, in fields such as parapsychology, is treated as heresy by the scientific community, according to Peter A. Sturrock. In the following viewpoint, he argues that advances in scientific knowledge begin with curiosity and creative thinking about anomalies. These anomalies, including the so-called paranormal, are then amenable to scientific study, he maintains. Sturrock is a professor of space science and astrophysics at Stanford University and is president of the Society for Scientific Exploration.

As you read, consider the following questions:

1. How does Sturrock define "pathological science"?
2. According to the author, how was Galileo's model of the universe a challenge to the church?
3. In the author's opinion, in what two ways can a strong case for a new proposition be built?

Edward Ginzton, one of the founders of Varian Associates, once remarked, concerning his colleague Russell Varian, that "he had several modes of thought, of which logical thinking was only one." So it is, most likely, with all great inventors, and so it is, I believe, with all truly productive scientists. In this viewpoint, I will argue that scientists need at least three modes of thought that I call "curious," "creative" and "critical."

AN ANOMALY IN ASTRONOMY

These requirements, though they may be quite general in their applicability, come sharply into focus when one deals with anomalies within mainstream science or with anomalous phenomena that seem to reside outside of science as we know it. Let us take just one example from within mainstream science. It has been claimed for some years by Halton Arp of Munich and by William Tifft of the Steward Observatory in Tucson, Arizona, that there is evidence indicating that our interpretation of the redshifts of astronomical objects is incomplete. [The wavelength of light from distant objects lengthens, shifting toward the red end of the spectrum, as they and the Earth move away from each other—ed.] Their results, if taken at face value, contradict the usual assumption that the redshift of distant objects (such as distant galaxies and quasars) is due almost entirely to the expansion of the universe. Arp and Tifft have been curious in examining strange patterns that arose in their early observations; they have also been creative in trying to seek an interpretation of their results; and they have been critical of their own work by seeking new observations and encouraging others to make independent observations.

Then what is the problem? It is that the astronomical community has, by and large, applied only critical thinking to the same problem. There have been some attempts to reproduce Tifft's results, with mixed success, but the general attitude has been, "It cannot happen, therefore it does not happen," just the opposite of good advice once given by the great physicist Robert Leighton of the California Institute of Technology, "If it does happen, it can happen." As a result of this attitude, Arp and Tifft have come to be regarded somewhat as heretics. Indeed, Arp lost his observing privileges at the Mount Wilson and Palomar Observatories, forcing him to leave the United States to go to his present home in Germany.

An even more disturbing and challenging situation arises if a scientist takes an interest in a topic that is outside of mainstream science and is believed by the scientific community to represent "pseudoscience," the "paranormal," or "pathological science." Some of the best known examples that are regarded in this light are "parapsychology," "ufology" (the study of UFO reports) and "cryptozoology" (the search for zoological anomalies, including "Big Foot" and the so-called "Loch Ness Monster"). Even the mention of such terms will send a shudder through the frame of almost any self-respecting scientist. Why is this so?

Typical responses to this question are in fact indicated by the terms I have just used. If I assert that a subject is "pseudoscience," I am stating that the activity is not truly scientific but merely pretends to be scientific. However, such an assertion is indefensible. A "subject" is neither scientific nor nonscientific. It is only the study carried out by a particular person or group of persons that can be so described. One may be able to make a legitimate case that this person who studies parapsychology is being pseudoscientific, but that does not mean that it is impossible for some other person to carry out a study in the same field that meets the highest standards of the scientific enterprise.

There is a similar problem connected with the term "paranormal." If I assert that a subject is "paranormal," I am implying that I know what is "normal." I am further implying that any subject that is not "normal," according to my definition of the term, does not accord with scientific knowledge and must be rejected as bogus. This would be a huge responsibility to take on. If pressed on this issue, most scientists would agree that science is incomplete. They would agree with Isaac Newton who stated that he felt like a boy "finding a smoother pebble or a prettier shell than ordinary, whilst the great ocean of truth lay all undiscovered before me." If we do not know all there is to know about the universe (including human beings and everything else in the universe), then clearly we cannot claim to know what is "normal," and it is therefore foolish to use the term "paranormal."

On the other hand, the term "pathological science" is somewhat more useful. It refers to poor, slipshod and misleading research that yields results that turn out to be false. However, the term was originally coined by the Nobel Laureate Irving Langmuir to imply that certain fields are made up only of bad science. If this were the case (an assertion that is in itself debatable), it would prove only that better work needs to be done, not that such fields should be placed off-limits to scientific research.

THE SCIENTIFIC COMMUNITY

In thinking about such questions over the years, I have come to the conclusion that the problem with such topics is not a purely intellectual difficulty in trying to understand the nature of the phenomenon or to assess the quality and conclusions of the research. I have concluded that the key to the puzzle is to be found in nonscientific and nonintellectual considerations. Although the prototype of a scientist is that of a lone researcher following the truth according to his own light, with little heed to the world around him, such is not the scientist that we know today, and perhaps the image was never more than a myth. Science today is a collective enterprise. Much of the work is done in groups. Even an individual scientist is dependent upon the good will and support of his fellow scientists for the wherewithal to continue his work. Furthermore, the activities of science are supported by, and to some extent controlled by, organizations such as scientific societies, agencies of the federal government and (to a lesser but nonnegligible extent) by the structuring of universities and corporations into schools, divisions, departments, laboratories, etc. These organizations in turn need the respect and support of the public, and they need favorable press from the news media. Any scientist who jeopardizes the good standing of these important scientific organizations may, knowingly or unknowingly, weaken organized science and thereby hurt his fellow scientists. In this way, the issue is converted from one that is purely intellectual to one that has sociological and political consequences. Such issues are perceived as heretical precisely because they involve a combination of intellectual and political considerations.

SCIENCE AND HERESY

My understanding of the term "heresy" is the following: *A heresy is a proposition that is, at the same time, a challenge to understanding and a challenge to power.* Galileo faced the investigators of the Holy Inquisition in 1633 as a result of his assertion that the Ptolemaic model of the solar system, in which the Earth is at rest and all bodies revolve around the Earth, is wrong, and that the Copernican model (the creation of a Protestant!) that places the Sun at the center and has the Earth revolve around the Sun is correct. Perhaps more important was his implicit assertion that we may discover truth about the universe by observation rather than through the reading of Holy Scripture. In addition to the purely intellectual challenge of offering a new model of the solar system, Galileo was challenging the Church as the ultimate arbiter of truth. Galileo was thereby challenging the status and power of the Church.

Similarly, in their assertions, Arp and Tifft are challenging the status and power of astronomers who have based their study of the structure of the universe on the assumption that the redshift of galaxies and quasars is a measure of their distance. These astronomers may legitimately fear that, if Arp and Tifft prove to be correct, much of present-day astronomical research—including their own research—will be destined for the dustbin.

RESISTANCE TO THE FINDINGS OF PARAPSYCHOLOGY

As you know, the scientific establishment in general pays no attention to the findings of parapsychology. They are almost never taught as part of a scientific or even a general education. Most scientists (and laymen and religious professionals) can honestly say they have seen no evidence to make them take the field seriously. . . . Part of the *implicit* education of scientists is the occasional disparaging remark about what nonsense parapsychology is. We want social acceptance, to belong, so we don't look at the evidence and then can indeed honestly say that we have never seen anything to convince us!

Charles T. Tart, *ReVision*, Summer 1995.

One may discern a similar conflict in relation to fields such as parapsychology. The very term "parapsychology" is unfortunate, since it gives the misleading impression that it is somehow related to "psychology," thereby implying that psychologists should know whether or not there is anything to this subject. Since psychologists, in fact, know very little about parapsychology, this creates a situation of some tension. If it turns out that the claims of parapsychologists are correct, and that the human mind has abilities that are not now understood on the basis of 20th century science, organized psychology will (fairly or unfairly) suffer something of a setback. One can imagine that the public and the news media will implicitly or explicitly criticize the psychological community for not realizing early on that there was something to parapsychology. The psychological community would, to some extent, lose face. Hence the current conflict between parapsychology investigators and organized psychology is not unlike the conflict between Galileo and the Church. Whether or not these investigators will prove to be correct in their assertions, as Galileo has been proved to be correct, remains to be seen, but the ultimate truth or falsity of a proposition is not, in my opinion, a relevant consideration in trying to determine whether or not a challenge is a heresy.

Of course, some important challenges are not regarded as

heresies at all. For instance, it was a major intellectual challenge to try to understand the nature of pulsars or of quasars when they were first discovered. However, these discoveries were made by world-class scientists, at prestigious universities, who were members of the scientific establishment. Far from being perceived as a demonstration of the shortcomings of the establishment, they were hailed as shining examples of what the establishment does that is right. Far from weakening organized science, these discoveries help to cement the power of those organizations and of science in general.

CURIOUS AND CREATIVE THINKING

In summary, I claim that in trying to understand topics that get an emotional reaction from scientists, it is first essential that we understand the reason for the emotional reaction. Only when one is past that point can one move on to a more rational consideration of these topics: the way to advance curious, creative and critical thinking is to remove the hidden obstacles to such thinking.

Even when the nonintellectual barriers are removed, there can still be some confusion about the nature of scientific investigation. One may detect in some discussions the implicit assumption that scientific knowledge is absolute. The term "law" promotes such a belief, but a scientific "law" is not an absolute and immutable truth; indeed, it may be more accurate to regard it simply as a shorthand summary of the results of observations and experiments carried out to date. Further observation or new experiments may show that the "law" must be revised if not rescinded.

Science advances by trial and error. Linda Pauling, daughter of the famous chemist Linus Pauling, once asked her father, "How is it you had so many good ideas?" to which he replied, "I had many more ideas, and threw away all the bad ones." With luck, a scientist can recognize a bad idea very quickly, hopefully before he or she publishes. However, some ideas prove to be wrong or, expressed more charitably, "less than universal in their applicability," only after centuries of research. It took 300 years for Newtonian dynamics to be superseded by relativity and quantum mechanics. Who is to say that relativity and quantum mechanics will not, in their turn, at some time be superseded by a more intricate and subtle theory of which we now have no conception?

It is obvious that, if we wish to learn something new, we should be curious. However, curiosity is not enough. To conceive of a pattern or law or theory, one must make an unjustified leap beyond the evidence. Newton's proposal of a universal law of gravity was simply a guess—but an inspired guess, one that was confirmed by many subsequent observations and analyses. Even so, the guess proved eventually to be not quite right and to require modification by Einstein and others. "Creation" is simply inspired guesswork.

CRITICAL THINKING

It is only after curiosity and creativity have done their work that critical thinking should come into play. At this stage, it is essential to cast a stern critical eye on one's latest act of creation. (We may count upon our colleagues to help us wholeheartedly in this activity.) However, it is essential that criticism be even-handed: it should be applied to old ideas as well as to new ideas. As the astrophysicist Tommy Gold once remarked, "Old ideas are not right simply because they are old, and new ideas are not wrong simply because they are new." In facing any new proposition, one brings to it years of observation, learning—and perhaps indoctrination. As a human being, one may feel "this idea is so preposterous that I do not even want to consider the evidence," but as a scientist one should state "this proposition seems very unlikely, and it will take a lot of evidence to persuade me to take it seriously." Carl Sagan was correct in asserting that "extraordinary claims require extraordinary evidence," but that does not mean that anything less than extraordinary evidence may be ignored. We learn from the study of scientific inference that a strong case for a new proposition can be built either from one very strong piece of evidence or from the combination of a number of independent and less spectacular pieces of evidence. In science, as in real life, one may get from point A to point B either in one giant leap or by a number of small steps—either by flying or by walking.

We should also remember that evidence that appears resistant to understanding and to require an "extraordinary claim" may, when viewed from a different—perhaps broader—perspective, prove to be comprehensible in terms of existing scientific knowledge, or only a slight rearrangement of that knowledge. An example is the story of meteorites. These were impossible to understand when they were viewed simply as "stones falling from the sky," because the sky does not contain stones. However, when they were viewed as objects arriving from outer space, the difficulty evaporated. This simple change of perspective came about largely as the result of a very thorough investigation, by the great French scientist Jean-Batiste Biot, of a dramatic meteorite fall that occurred in L'Aigle, France, in 1803. It may prove that only a slight broadening of our present perspective will make it possible to comprehend some of the phenomena that now seem "extraordinary."

SCIENCE AND PARAPSYCHOLOGY

However, there is no doubt that there now exists something of a no-man's-land between organized science on the one hand and the public and news media on the other hand, an area that contains topics such as parapsychology, ufology and cryptozoology. The public is curious and wants answers to these questions. The average citizen does not have the skills necessary to resolve these mysteries. The scientific community has a store of knowledge and an arsenal of techniques that could be brought to bear on these problems, but this is not happening because the scientific community views these subjects as being "off-limits." Such topics are "beyond the pale."

The Society for Scientific Exploration was founded in 1982 to help redress this situation. The Society offers a forum, through its meetings and through its journal, the *Journal of Scientific Exploration*, for the presentation of the results of serious investigations into any topic amenable to such investigation. All the topics mentioned in this viewpoint (and many more) have been discussed at our meetings and in our journal. There have, to date, been no major breakthroughs in the sense of research that establishes the reality and nature of any of these phenomena. On the other hand, our knowledge is improving and our insight is increasing. It is my conviction that, if we persevere with the judicious application of curious, creative and critical thinking, it will be only a matter of time before each of these enigmas is finally resolved.

"Film and television entertainment
programming increasingly portrays
science and reason as tools that are
unsuitable for understanding our
world in a new age of credulity."

TELEVISION SHOWS ABOUT THE PARANORMAL ARE ANTISCIENTIFIC

William Evans

Television shows that portray paranormal phenomena have become very popular. In the following viewpoint, William Evans
contends that these new films and television shows portray the
paranormal as normal, and they characterize scientists and skeptics as impediments to solving paranormal problems. He argues
that such programs do not merely promote belief in the paranormal, they create hostility toward science, skepticism, and the
scientific method. Evans is an assistant professor of communications at Georgia State University in Atlanta.

As you read, consider the following questions:

1. According to Evans, what views of science and scientists are
   habitual television watchers more likely to hold than
   infrequent viewers?
2. According to the author, how does Hollywood most
   frequently portray skeptics?
3. In the author's opinion, why is the total immersion of The
   X-Files in the paranormal worrisome?

From William Evans, "Science and Reason in Film and Television," Skeptical Inquirer,
January/February 1996. Reprinted by permission of the Committee for the Scientific
Investigation of Claims of the Paranormal.

W ho has the most dangerous job on prime-time entertainment television? The police officer? The soldier? The private investigator? The answer is "none of the above." On prime-time entertainment television, scientists are most at risk. Ten percent of scientists featured in prime-time entertainment programming get killed, and five percent kill someone. No other occupational group is more likely to kill or be killed.

Popular entertainment media have long portrayed scientists as mad, bad, and dangerous to know, but in the past few decades entertainment media portrayals of science have changed significantly, and these changes seem to have accelerated in recent years. Science remains dangerous, but it is also increasingly portrayed as useless in solving problems. The skepticism about paranormal claims that is a part of scientific thinking is portrayed as a handicap. And in many newer entertainment media offerings—most notably in "The X-Files"—the paranormal is portrayed as, well, normal. "The X-Files" offers a world in which fantastic events such as alien abductions and spontaneous human combustion are everyday occurrences.

Film and television entertainment programming increasingly portrays science and reason as tools that are unsuitable for understanding our world in a new age of credulity. This viewpoint reviews entertainment media portrayals of science and pseudoscience and considers the important function of skepticism in horror films and other offerings. The evidence reported here will likely be discouraging for many skeptics, but it is evidence that skeptics must nonetheless consider if they are to effectively counter entertainment media tendencies to devalue science and reason.

TELEVISION AND PUBLIC CONCEPTIONS OF SCIENCE

There is a correlation between watching entertainment television and credulity. Habitual viewers of entertainment television—approximately one-third of U.S. adults watch more than four hours of television daily—are more likely than infrequent viewers to hold negative opinions about science and positive opinions about pseudoscience. Habitual viewers are more likely than infrequent viewers to believe that science is dangerous, that scientists are odd and peculiar people, and that a career in science is undesirable. These findings persist even taking into consideration education, sex, age, and other factors that are known to influence people's attitudes toward science. Habitual viewers are also more likely than infrequent viewers to believe that astrology is scientific. Thirty-seven percent of adults in the United

States believe that astrology is scientific, but among habitual viewers of television this figure is 55 percent.

While the existing evidence does not permit us to claim that viewing entertainment television creates antiscience and pro-pseudoscience attitudes, it seems certain that entertainment television provides a symbolic environment in which such attitudes are readily cultivated. Our entertainment mass media provide a steady diet of negative images of science and skepticism—images that reflect and reinforce popular misgivings and misunderstandings about science.

MAD SCIENTISTS AND CLEVER LAYPERSONS

Western literature and popular entertainment media have long featured scientists in the role of the troublemaker. Mad scientists are second only to psychotics as the primary source of trouble in horror films. In fact, mad scientists account for a larger percentage of horror movie antagonists than zombies, werewolves, and mummies combined.

Although scientists have been consistently portrayed as dangerous in twentieth-century popular entertainment media, there have been important changes in the portrayal of scientists' abilities to solve problems. Andrew Tudor, author of *Monsters and Mad Scientists*, notes that between 1951 and 1964 scientists were often portrayed in film as being responsible for saving as well as endangering humanity. In films of that era science is dangerous, but science also provides the most appropriate means of dealing with the dangers that science unleashes. Scientists might, for example, inadvertently create mutant monsters, but scientists also most commonly figure out how to eliminate the threats they have created. In these films, science is dangerous but efficacious.

In contrast, more recent entertainment films portray scientists as being unable to solve problems or eliminate threats to humanity. Instead, laypersons most commonly save the day. Scientific expertise is devalued in these films, and may even be portrayed as a handicap of sorts. In horror films like *C.H.U.D.* and the 1988 remake of *The Blob*, laypersons rid the world of dangerous creatures, but only after the laypersons outwit scientists who either fail to understand the dangers or who have a vested interest in perpetuating the dangers. In films like *E.T.* and *Splash*, laypersons save the lives of kind and intelligent creatures by rescuing them from scientific captivity. In these and many other recent films, science no longer provides resources for solving problems, but rather, becomes an obstacle to solving problems.

Like science, skepticism is devalued in current popular film and entertainment television. Indeed, skepticism is shown to be untenable and even irresponsible. Films about the paranormal typically feature a fictional skeptical character who doubts the reality of poltergeists, demons, and other paranormal phenomena, even though it quickly becomes apparent to everyone else—story characters and audience alike—that supernatural forces are at work. As a result of the skeptic's refusal to acknowledge the reality of the supernatural, the film's protagonists are endangered. These films typically include a pivotal scene in which the protagonists explicitly reject the skeptical point of view. Soon after, the skeptic is either killed, converted to credulity, or simply written out of the action. At this point in the film, the protagonists (who, again, are seldom scientists unless they have "converted" to credulity) can eliminate the paranormal threat.

TELEVISION REINFORCES BELIEF IN THE PARANORMAL

Polls show that superstition and belief in the supernatural are still powerful forces in the national psyche. And the proliferation of television shows that cater to that spooky sensibility—including "Unsolved Mysteries," "The X-Files" and NBC's new show "The Other Side"—only reinforce the pseudoscientific underpinnings of such beliefs.

John Schwartz, *Washington Post*, October 31, 1994.

A quintessential example of this narrative structure is found in the film *Poltergeist III*. In this fictional story, a psychologist, Dr. Seaton, steadfastly insists that young Carol Anne is not being pursued by demons, but rather, is suffering from an emotional disturbance of some sort. Dr. Seaton continues to insist that nothing supernatural is going on long after he, every other major character in the movie, and the movie audience have seen quite remarkable supernatural events. Dr. Seaton's diagnosis is clearly wrong, but as a skeptic he is unwilling to accept the ample evidence of supernatural forces at work. As a result, Carol Anne suffers repeated and terrifying encounters with otherworldly entities. Dr. Seaton seems cruel, and his continued skepticism in the face of incontrovertible evidence seems almost pathological.

Fortunately for Carol Anne, a psychic arrives to save her. The psychic, named Tangina, becomes aware of Carol Anne's plight via telepathy and rushes to help her, only to be rebuked and ridiculed by Dr. Seaton. As the peril to Carol Anne and others grows, and Dr. Seaton refuses to accept Tangina's warnings about the great power of supernatural forces, Tangina demands that Carol Anne's uncle and aunt (with whom Carol Anne is living) make a choice: They must choose between Tangina's mysticism and Dr. Seaton's rationalism. The uncle and aunt decide to follow Tangina's recommendations and to reject Dr. Seaton's counsel. When Dr. Seaton objects, the previously restrained uncle treats him harshly, calling the psychologist's diagnoses "stupid and idiotic." The outcome of this confrontation is meant to be pleasing to an audience that has witnessed Dr. Seaton's increasingly strained and, finally ludicrous, attempts to find prosaic explanations for fantastic events. Shortly after this confrontation, Dr. Seaton is killed, pushed down an elevator shaft by a teenager who is possessed by evil spirits. At this point, the real work of saving Carol Anne can begin, and sure enough it is a combination of faith and benevolent psychic power that in the end save Carol Anne and her loved ones from the malevolent spirits.

FILM PORTRAYALS OF SKEPTICS

While the portrayal of Dr. Seaton is perhaps unusually negative, skeptics are frequency portrayed by Hollywood as being dogmatic, misanthropic, and just plain wrong. In films such as Poltergeist III, The Entity, and even Ghostbusters (where the skeptic is the U.S. Environmental Protection Agency official who insists that it is the ghostbusters rather than ghosts who are responsible for an epidemic of strange phenomena and whose order to shut down the ghostbusters' "containment system" brings predictable, dire consequences), skepticism is shown to be foolish and inefficacious, while psychics and parapsychologists step in to eliminate the paranormal threats.

David. J. Hess, author of Science in the New Age, and Tudor identify the transition from skepticism to credulity as a major theme and distinguishing feature of recent horror and suspense movies. People who live in haunted houses (e.g., as in The Amityville Horror), or find their loved ones possessed or pursued by demons (e.g., The Exorcist, Poltergeist), or find themselves immersed in satanic conspiracies (e.g., Rosemary's Baby, The Omen) typically are at first skeptical regarding the supernatural; but their safety and even their survival require that they acknowledge the reality of the supernatural. In these films, to deny the reality of the supernatural is to place oneself and one's loved ones at risk. As audience members, we often find ourselves rooting for skeptical characters to forsake skepticism. Sometimes a converted skeptic must work to convert other skeptics, to make others recognize the reality and danger of the supernatural. Here again, audience members often find themselves rooting for successful evangelization, since the survival of one or more likable characters, and perhaps even the world, depends on it. The power of these narratives is such that even dedicated skeptics often find themselves cheering when a skeptical character comes to believe in the supernatural.

THE PARANORMAL BECOMES NORMAL

While skeptics should be distressed by films that portray the transition from skepticism to credulity as a matter of life and death, at least these films acknowledge that skepticism is an understandable first response to fantastic claims and wondrous events. In these films, the major characters typically at first consider prosaic explanations, even though they soon become convinced that supernatural forces are at work. These films reassure us that the major characters are not eager to believe in the supernatural, that they are sensible, normal people. (In fact, very few mainstream entertainment media offerings portray the victims of the supernatural as having had an interest in the supernatural before they became victims, even though in the real world a previous interest in UFOs, demons, and other paranormal phenomena is characteristic of those who claim to have encountered such phenomena.)

In contrast to entertainment media offerings in which skepticism is portrayed as a normal, if untenable, response to fantastic claims, the television series "The X-Files" presents a new and potentially pernicious portrayal of the paranormal as entirely normal. In "The X-Files," FBI agents Fox Mulder and Dana Scully investigate paranormal events in the same routinized, "it's all in a day's work" manner in which "Dragnet's" Sergeant Friday and Officer Gannon investigated armed robbery and petty theft. Paranormal events are mundane, "The X-Files" suggests, and even an initial but quickly abandoned skepticism is no longer warranted. Agent Mulder is always ready (and often eager) to consider the possibility that paranormal forces account for the phenomena he is investigating, and his hunches typically prove to be correct. In conversation, Mulder and other characters are fond of offering offhand and even wholly gratuitous, credulous references to a wide variety of paranormal phenomena. C. Eugene Emery Jr. aptly characterizes these references as "extraneous poppycock."

Agent Scully plays "The X-Files'" token skeptic, but as Emery notes, Scully's skepticism is often a symptom of her closed-mindedness. Like Dr. Seaton in *Poltergeist* III, Scully remains skeptical even after she has witnessed remarkable and unequivocally paranormal events. Her skepticism is seldom shown to be useful or warranted, and in later episodes she seems decidedly less skeptical (a change that should perhaps be expected given the many paranormal forces and extraterrestrial beings she has encountered in the show's first two seasons).

THE "X-FILES" BELIEVERS

"The X-Files" achieves a kind of realism that sets it apart from previous television science fiction series such as "The Twilight Zone" and "The Outer Limits." "The X-Files" adopts the quasi-documentary style of recent television police dramas, appropriates the authority and prestige of the Federal Bureau of Investigation, and suggests that "The X-Files" cases are similar to real cases. "The X-Files" perhaps has more in common with shows such as "Unsolved Mysteries" and "Sightings"—shows in which allegedly real paranormal events are often reenacted—than it does with older shows such as "The Twilight Zone." In following the discussions of "The X-Files" fans on the Internet, it becomes clear that, while most fans do not believe "The X-Files" to be a documentary (although a few fans seem to have trouble distinguishing fact from fiction), many believe that "The X-Files" cases are highly plausible and that the FBI and other government agencies are actively, if secretly, investigating similar cases.

In popular entertainment prior to "The X-Files," skepticism was necessary, if only to provide an obstacle for the protagonists to overcome. In "The X-Files," skepticism is almost wholly unnecessary. Although it remains to be seen if future entertainment media offerings will follow the lead of "The X-Files," the total immersion of "The X-Files" in the paranormal is worrisome. It suggests that paranormal events are common and that even likable, educated, and attractive people like agents Mulder and Scully can embrace the supernatural.

SKEPTICISM AND HOLLYWOOD

Skeptics have had some success in persuading journalists to include a skeptical point of view in news stories about the paranormal, although, clearly, more needs to be done in this regard. Unfortunately, Hollywood accords skeptics no standing to address the portrayal (or the absence) of skepticism in film and television. Many film and television producers would no doubt claim that because their products are merely entertainment, neither viewers nor researchers should take "The X-Files" and similar offerings seriously. But this excuse is increasingly disingenuous as the evidence mounts that viewers' conceptions of reality are influenced by media entertainment programming. These same producers increasingly turn to docudramas, "reality-based" shows, tabloid journalism, and other program formats that owe their success in part to the strategic blurring of fact and fiction.

Hollywood television producers have agreed in recent years to work with experts to design portrayals that inform viewers about various health and environmental issues. Perhaps entertainment television and film producers can be recruited by scientists and skeptics to help ensure that critical thinking does not disappear from our entertainment media environment. Of course, it is perhaps easier to remind viewers that unprotected sex is dangerous or that aluminum cans can be recycled than it is to invite viewers to develop critical thinking habits, an invitation that would require producers to abandon their reliance on skepticism as a source of error and danger.

Carl Sagan implores television producers to work with scientists and skeptics to develop a nonfiction series that details how fantastic claims can be investigated scientifically—a kind of "Solved Mysteries." Such a series, Sagan suggests, could make for entertaining television that would also encourage viewers to appreciate and cultivate the power of rational thought and rigorous investigation. Unfortunately, although many viewers would find such a series worthwhile, it may never reach an audience watching tabloid television. As a culture, we have long preferred that our tales of the supernatural be credulous rather than skeptical. Still, the breathless celebration of the paranormal in current films and television programs must be addressed. Understanding the need for media portrayals of skepticism is a necessary first step toward change. Skeptics would do well to identify or invent commercially viable alternatives, and entertainment media producers would do well to more often and more explicitly acknowledge in their programming the important roles of science and reason in maintaining our civilization.

> "Television, the medium that affects
> our attitudes as a nation more than
> any other, can end up being the
> avatar of a truly New Age."

TELEVISION SHOWS ABOUT THE PARANORMAL ARE NOT ANTISCIENTIFIC

Loyd Auerbach

In the following viewpoint, Loyd Auerbach reviews a number of past and present television shows about the paranormal and says that some have presented parapsychology, UFOs, and similar phenomena in a more realistic manner than others. He argues that shows depicting the paranormal are appearing on television more frequently because the general public is interested in alternative ideas and the networks have realized the potential for such programs. Auerbach is a consulting editor of *Fate*, a monthly magazine that explores the paranormal.

As you read, consider the following questions:

1. In Auerbach's opinion, what differentiates the television show *Unsolved Mysteries* from other shows?
2. What has been the most popular paranormal topic on *ABC News*, according to the author?
3. What is the first reason listed by the author for the increase in paranormal programming?

From Loyd Auerbach, "Paranormal Programming Invades Prime Time," FATE Magazine, November 1994; ©1994 FATE Magazine, PO Box 64383, St. Paul, MN 55164-0383. Reprinted by permission.

I have been an avid television viewer for as long as I can remember. Coming from a family in which my father and an
uncle worked for major networks and a second uncle for a radio
station in New York, I was immersed in media even before I was
born. In fact, it was TV's influence that led me into parapsychological studies.

Series like *One Step Beyond*, John Newland's 1960s show, provided dramatizations of factual psychic experiences, great actors,
and believable scenarios. A true-life *Twilight Zone*, *One Step Beyond*
gave the impression of psychic reality. Newland also, from time
to time, broke from the traditional dramatization format, with
experts' discussions of the phenomena. One particularly well-
done episode, entitled "The Sacred Mushroom," featured Newland accompanying a team to meet with a brujo in Mexico,
where the team consumed mushrooms that purportedly gave
them enhanced psi ability for a time. The show continued in the
States with Newland eating a mushroom, then being tested for
ESP (something clearly illegal now).

While other shows occasionally dealt with psychics and psychic ability back then, Newland's certainly set the groundwork
for future coverage of the topic. *One Step Beyond* can be seen on the
Sci-Fi Channel, as well as on video (selected episodes have been
released on VHS tape).

Many fictional dramas such as *Dark Shadows* dealt heavily with
the supernatural and occasionally included psi abilities and paranormal scenarios (from *Star Trek* to *The Champions*). Another series
that presented an exploration of phenomena had a parapsychologist as the main character. The show was *The Sixth Sense*.

A Sampling of Paranormal Television

The Sixth Sense, a one-hour drama (currently airing in syndication
as half-hour, poorly edited episodes of *Night Gallery*), starred Gary
Collins as parapsychologist Michael Rhodes. While the show included some fairly accurate presentations of the ESP experiments
of the time, Rhodes himself was presented as a parapsychologist
with psi abilities, and the storylines of the episodes were less
than realistic. Unfortunately, this series gave a good part of the
viewing audience the idea that all parapsychologists were also
psychics (not true, alas). Still, the show did bring the field into
the public eye, if only for a short time.

Then there was *Kolchak: The Night Stalker*. In 1971 Darren Mc-
Gavin first played oddball journalist Carl Kolchak in the TV vam-
pire movie *The Night Stalker*. That film (out on video) became the
highest-rated TV movie up to that time and led ABC to air a se-

quel, *The Night Strangler*, in 1973. A year later, ABC aired a 20-episode series. The films were written by horror/TV writer Richard Matheson and produced and directed by Dan Curtis (*Dark Shadows*). By the way, the novel the first film was based on and a novel based on the second film, both by Jeff Rice, recently have been re-released.

The show was wild, imaginative, fun and, unfortunately, stuck in a bad time slot. So, many of us have only fond memories of Carl Kolchak, but we do have other shows to look forward to. In fact, one of the current shows I will discuss owes much to Kolchak and his hunt for wild phenomena and horrible creatures. . . .

THE FIRST OF THE NEW PARANORMAL SHOWS

In 1988 the predecessor of most reality TV premiered on NBC and has been running ever since. *Unsolved Mysteries*, hosted by Robert Stack, takes to heart (and mind) people's interest in all kinds of mysteries. The show focuses on a wide range of events and unsolved circumstances, from ghosts and poltergeists to missing persons cases, from twins separated at birth living parallel lives to murderers on the loose.

Unsolved Mysteries, produced and created by John Cosgrove and Terry Dunn Meurer, has set a tone for reality TV by including both interviews with real participants in the events covered and brief recreations of the events (unfortunately, often with less than outstanding actors).

While *Unsolved Mysteries* presents paranormal topics, what differentiates it from other shows is its mixture of often unrelated topics, making it a more eclectic reality TV show.

In the fall of 1991, the FOX TV network aired a special on UFOs. This was the first *Sightings*, in a format created by TV producer and UFO enthusiast Linda Moulton Howe. It was successful enough for FOX to order two other specials—in February 1992, one on ghosts, and in May 1992, one on powers of the mind. All three specials were successful, enabling FOX to try *Sightings* as a weekly series.

Produced by Henry Winkler and Ann Daniel, *Sightings* was hosted by Tim White, a FOX TV news anchor, who did an excellent job of fronting the show. Highly rated for a FOX Friday evening show, its performance seemed to lag towards the final episodes. Along with the ratings deterioration, there was a general shift in the content and quality of the episodes. Finally, *Sightings* was canceled in spring of 1993—but wait—it's coming back.

THE X-FILES: MONSTERS AND CONSPIRACIES

In fall 1993 a new kind of paranormal show appeared in the old *Sightings* time slot on Fridays. A bit of a sleeper in popularity and ratings, *The X-Files*, created and produced by Chris Carter for FOX, presented the paranormal, the supernatural, and UFOs in a dramatic context. Owing much of its ancestry to *Kolchak:The Night Stalker* (according to Carter), *The X-Files* follows the adventures of FBI agents Fox Mulder (David Duchovny) and Dana Scully (Gillian Anderson), who are placed in situations that Mulder embraces and Scully approaches skeptically (though that skepticism has waned heavily over the course of the first season's run of episodes).

BELIEF IN THE PARANORMAL

Do you believe:

	Yes	Not Sure	No
1. In miracles?	79%	9%	12%
2. In angels?	72	13	15
3. That people can hear from or communicate mentally with someone who has died?	28	21	51
4. In reincarnation—that is, the rebirth of the soul in a new body after death?	27	20	53
5. In astrology?	23	16	61

	Very likely	Somewhat Likely	Unlikely	Not Sure
6. That flying saucers are real?	19%	30.7%	43.1%	7.3%

Note: Percentages do not add up to 100 due to rounding.

Sources: CNN *USA Today*/Gallup Poll, based on nationwide random telephone survey of 1,016 adults over age 18, conducted December 16–18, 1994 (questions 1–5); Scripps Howard News Service/Ohio University poll, based on nationwide random telephone survey of 1,006 people, June 1995 (question 6).

While the FBI doesn't really have cases like *The X-Files* (that we know of), the characters and settings of the show are presented to give the impression that these could be real events. With UFO abductions, satanic cults, mass and bizarre murderers, and bodies giving off toxic fumes in the headlines these days, *The X-Files* merely reflects much of the popular interest in the unusual and bizarre and our fascination with things we should be afraid of. The show also has dealt with science fiction monsters, DNA manipulation, natural mutations, prehistoric insects awakened from hibernation, and sex-shifting aliens (who are also psychic vampires). These topics give this show a very different feel than its predecessors had.

Add in government conspiracies that even these intrepid FBI agents can't get a handle on without help from an anonymous government informant (who died in the first season's finale), and watching this show can really give you the creeps. And unlike lovable Carl Kolchak, who you knew was always going to get his monster, however clumsily, by the end of the episode, Mulder and Scully have been injured on different episodes, and there is always the sense that they may fail in their quest.

It looked for a time like FOX might cancel The X-Files early in the first year, but there seemed to be a shift in attitude (maybe an alien influence?), and there appeared to be an increase in the number of promotions on FOX (and in other venues) for the show. The ratings grew as more people tried the show out, and now there are even X-Files aficionados grouping together on the Internet.

ON-LINE X-FILES

It was recently announced that an X-Files forum will be accessible on line through Delphi Internet Services Corp., recently purchased by FOX's owner, Rupert Murdoch. On-line users will be able to report their own strange experiences, interact in discussions about the programs with Chris Carter and other show producers and writers, and download an episode guide, background data about the show, and even photos.

Has The X-Files had an impact on other TV? Some new paranormal programs were in the development stage even while X-Files was starting up, but it seems clear that Sightings' track record, when multiplied by the success of The X-Files, has fully opened the doors for other paranormal programming.

FOX followed its previous Sightings success with a UFO special in February 1994 and a short summer series entitled Encounters: The Hidden Truth. Produced by the Berkeley Group, originally part of the team that produced the first Sightings, this short-run series dealt heavily with UFOs and hidden evidence, tossing in a few other paranormal stories for good measure. Hosted by John Marshall, the show is on hiatus at the time of this writing. . . .

But what of the major networks? They're beginning to produce shows covering paranormal subjects, too.

Witness the number of UFO and paranormal stories that have appeared on network news programs like 20/20 and PrimeTime

Live (ABC). The most popular topics for ABC News seem to have been Near-Death Experiences and reincarnation/past life experiences, but angels, UFOs, and psychics have also been part of the programs.

While that network seems content to leave the anomalous to their news magazine shows, NBC and CBS have done specials over the past couple of years and are planning more. NBC aired a two-hour special on angels and a second one on alternative healing. CBS has done specials on ghosts and will have a Halloween special on the air (possibly already aired by the time you read this). . . .

The networks are also shopping for true-life ghost stories. I have been in discussion with three production companies about my past cases. Sadly, for TV movies they typically want a haunting where there is danger, either physical or emotional, and much fear. Nobody wants to watch a movie about a good ghost (except in the theaters, where movies like *Ghost* and *Hearts and Souls* seem to do well).

THE PARANORMAL IN SYNDICATION

Besides the network offerings, we need to look at what's happening in syndication. For those of you not TV savvy, a syndicated program is one offered to individual stations around the country. A show may air on any station in a given area, depending on who buys the rights to air it, whether a network affiliate or independent station. The best examples of such syndication are old TV shows rerun all over the world (like *Gilligan's Island*). Until a few years ago, the only new programming to be syndicated were game shows (like *Wheel of Fortune*). *Star Trek: The Next Generation* was the first of the truly successful first-run syndicated shows. Now we have quite a number of them: *Kung Fu*, *Babylon 5*, *Robocop*, and *BayWatch* are examples. Syndication also provides the viewing audience with paranormal programming. . . .

Of note is the reincarnation of *Sightings* in syndication. Not content to bring the show back as it was, executive producers Henry Winkler and Ann Daniel, along with co-executive producer Steve Kroopnick and coordinating producer Michelle Davis, will be presenting an all-new, one-hour weekly news magazine show with the tag line, according to Davis, "the truth lies beyond the imagination." The new *Sightings* . . . has been syndicated by Paramount Domestic Television to more than 145 stations, covering 85 per cent of the U.S. audience.

My conversations with Davis and segment producer Craig Armstrong have been very encouraging. The show, they tell me, will have a news magazine format that will expand well beyond the limited base that the show had while with FOX. Davis informed me that they "had little or no opportunity" to really present stories the way they should have been covered, and that there were a number of areas they wanted to get into but were unable to.

Segment producers have been assigned specific areas to deal with, a different approach than with previous magazine shows. This will enable them to become knowledgeable about the subject matter and present it in an informed fashion.

And the expanding base of topics? According to Davis and the press materials I received, *Sightings* will cover (besides UFOs, psychic phenomena, and monsters, their old topics) how people become psychics, the power of prayer in healing, encounters with angels, the Australian "Bermuda Triangle," spontaneous human combustion, the effects of Near-Death Experiences on people who came back, government cover-ups (not just of UFOs), places associated with spiritual power, new species of animals and insects still being discovered today, and even the Gaia theory and how it relates to consciousness. New science stories will also be covered as we move towards the 21st century. They also plan stories to range far from the U.S.

Good Stories

"So far," said Davis, "Paramount has been completely supportive of the good stories we want to present." The show is also not limited to a set number of segments; each piece will run from two to ten minutes, with a primary focus on active happenings or developing scenarios. The show will once again be hosted by Tim White.

How good will it be? You will know that before you have read this, provided you've tuned in to the show. . . .

But why this surge of paranormal and related programming? Why are the networks doing shows on angels and other previously pooh-poohed subjects? Because the viewing audience has finally become interested in these subjects.

Poll after poll over the past decade has shown that people are interested in alternative topics. More recently, marketing polls of TV audiences have supported this idea, and it has become clear that people will watch such subjects on TV week after week.

The success of *The X-Files* lent final support to this. So, to the producers and broadcasters, this is an area ripe for exploration (and exploitation).

There are a couple of reasons why we have seen the rise of so many programs of this nature.

First, this really is an untapped area. There are many subtopics to get into with psychic phenomena alone. This will also expand past reality TV programming to spill into the more dramatic programming and even into sitcoms.

Second, just as there are high percentages of audience members interested in the subject matter, so too are television people interested. The powers that be in the networks (and the sponsors) are seeing a potential market for their products and are therefore more willing to allow producers and writers to cover these topics.

WHY THE PUBLIC LIKES PARANORMAL ENTERTAINMENT

Finally, members of the general public, faced with too much reality in their daily lives, are looking for alternative ideas to effect change in their lives, explore their own selves, and provide an alternative to religious traditions and daily rituals.

People are dissatisfied with their jobs and, told that such stress is bad for them, may feel the need to change. People want to know there's more to human existence than what they normally see in their own lives.

Our leaders are telling us that this is the decade of change. Some people are expecting a change with the advent of the new century, or even the new millennium. Interest is rising in new ideas that can provide such change, whether mental or physical. Because these needs for change are being identified and spread to others, the need for more information in a variety of media has become evident and necessary.

That many of these ideas are not new by any means is beside the point (there *are* some new things, like UFOs and new developments in science). Television, the medium that affects our attitudes as a nation more than any other, can end up being the avatar of a truly New Age.

Can we have so many programs dealing with the paranormal and other alternative topics on TV at one time? Of course (witness the number of cop shows on TV at any one time). Will they all succeed? No, this is television, after all. Will they all be good? Not likely.

But as consumers, you can affect what is on TV. If you like a show, let the producers, the networks, and the sponsors know. If you think something is presenting a subject unfairly, tell them. This is how people have influenced television for decades.

Whether we're getting this new programming because of a market being identified or because the producers and broadcasters are somehow becoming enlightened, let's encourage this trend.

PERIODICAL BIBLIOGRAPHY

The following articles have been selected to supplement the diverse views presented in this chapter. Addresses are provided for periodicals not indexed in the *Readers' Guide to Periodical Literature*, the *Alternative Press Index*, the *Social Sciences Index*, or the *Index to Legal Periodicals and Books*.

Sharon Begley	"Is There Anything to It? Evidence, Please," *Newsweek*, July 8, 1996.
John Beloff	"The Skeptical Position: Is It Tenable?" *Skeptical Inquirer*, May/June 1995.
Richard Corliss	"Autopsy or Fraud-topsy?" *Time*, November 27, 1995.
Ralph Estling	"Faith in Science," *Skeptical Inquirer*, July/August 1996.
Kendrick Frazier	"So Human a Quest," *Humanist*, November/December 1995.
William Grey	"Philosophy and the Paranormal: Skepticism, Miracles, and Knowledge," *Skeptical Inquirer*, Spring 1994.
Lance Jaroff	"Weird Science," *Time*, May 15, 1995.
Paul Kurtz	"The New Skepticism," *Skeptical Inquirer*, Winter 1994.
Rick Marin	"Alien Invasion!" *Newsweek*, July 8, 1996.
New York Times	"They Shoot Down the Paranormal, U.F.O.'s and Other Flights of Fancy," July 7, 1996.
Carl Sagan	"The Variety of Supernatural Experience," *Natural History*, February 1996.
Glenn G. Sparks, Tricia Hansen, and Rani Shah	"Do Televised Depictions of Paranormal Events Influence Viewers' Beliefs?" *Skeptical Inquirer*, Summer 1994.
Martin Walker	"An Autopsy of the Third Kind," *World Press Review*, October 1995.
Richard Wiseman, Matthew Smith, and Jeff Wiseman	"Eyewitness Testimony and the Paranormal," *Skeptical Inquirer*, November/December 1995.

ARE UFOS
EXTRATERRESTRIAL
SPACECRAFT?

Chapter Preface

A 1995 survey by the Scripps-Howard News Service and Ohio University estimates that half of all American adults believe that unidentified flying objects (UFOs) are extraterrestrial spacecraft. Some people also claim to have had mysterious encounters with the alien occupants of these spaceships. Since the early 1980s, a few hundred "contactees" have reported being abducted by aliens, subjected to biological examinations, and forced to participate in the breeding of alien-human hybrid offspring. Skeptics have advanced a number of possible explanations for this phenomenon, including false memory syndrome, hypnagogic hallucinations (a sleep disorder), and outright hoaxes. But UFO researchers counter that these hypotheses do not adequately explain the phenomenon.

Stuart Appelle, a professor of psychology at the State University of New York, Brockport, and editor of the *Journal of UFO Studies*, is among those who maintain that at least some of the reports of alien abductions cannot be explained away as hoaxes or hallucinations. Investigations of various abductions have failed to show evidence that they are hoaxes or the products of unstable minds, he contends. Appelle further argues that the psychological explanations advanced by skeptics, such as false memory syndrome and hypnagogic hallucinations, have never been scientifically studied in relation to the alien abduction accounts. Therefore, he asserts, the hypothesis that some humans are literally being abducted by aliens is as viable as other explanations and should not be dismissed without scientific study.

Others, however, contend that the alien abduction accounts are too improbable to be believed. Jacques Vallee, an astrophysicist and computer scientist who has studied the UFO and alien abduction phenomena for many years, maintains that it is highly implausible that aliens are abducting humans for biological experiments. Genetic engineering techniques more advanced than the ones "abductees" report already exist within earthly science, he points out. If extraterrestrial visitors are technologically advanced enough to travel across vast distances of space, he argues, then they should be advanced enough to conduct biological experiments without the repeated abductions and painful procedures that experiencers report.

While many people believe that UFOs are extraterrestrial spaceships, fewer are willing to accept reports of alien abductions at face value. The viewpoints in the following chapter debate several questions concerning the probability of extraterrestrial visitors.

| "Every year, countless numbers of unidentified flying spacecraft are sighted, reported, and photographed."

UFOs Are Extraterrestrial Spacecraft

Alan Acree

Many people report seeing unidentified flying objects, and some believe these objects are extraterrestrial spacecraft. In the following viewpoint, Alan Acree takes issue with skeptics who contend that the phenomena can be explained as entirely earthly in origin. He argues that scientists should maintain open minds when examining evidence and should objectively consider the possibility that UFOs are extraterrestrial visitors. Acree is an English professor who lives in Indiana.

As you read, consider the following questions:

1. In the story of the campers told by Acree, how does John Kintz describe the UFO he saw?
2. What did the *La Grange Standard* say the unidentified flying object was, according to the author?
3. What is the author's response to skeptics looking for rock-solid evidence of UFOs?

From Alan Acree, "Unexplained Encounter," FATE Magazine, June 1996; ©1996 FATE Magazine, PO Box 64383, St. Paul, MN 55164-0383. Reprinted by permission.

As we rapidly approach the twenty-first century, technological advances seem to loom in the foreground. Nothing seems too futuristic or unobtainable. Even in today's modern world, however, some scholars, scientists, and authorities remain apprehensive or skeptical about the technological rationalization of certain unexplained phenomena—specifically, UFOs.

A plethora of nationwide UFO sightings have been reported and documented. These sightings are usually met with a certain skepticism and, in most cases, the witnesses have trouble proving their experiences' validity. Nevertheless, the fact remains that every year, countless numbers of unidentified flying spacecraft are sighted, reported, and photographed. The following account is an example.

INDIANA SIGHTING

Northeastern Indiana is not normally considered to be a UFO hot zone. The small town of Mongo, Indiana, sits quietly on the Pigeon River, and remains relatively peaceful year around, except for the bustling summer months when outdoor enthusiasts flock to enjoy the area's beautiful natural resources and to canoe and camp. The night of August 31, 1994, proved to be one of the most unsettling and controversial evenings of the entire summer.

On that clear August evening, at approximately 9:30 P.M., six men from Jackson, Michigan, were enjoying one of the last pleasant evenings of the summer. The Labor Day weekend was drawing to a close, bringing with it early traces of fall. The men were taking advantage of their holiday weekend by relaxing at the Trading Post Canoe Rental, a local canoe livery and campground nestled in the heart of the Pigeon River State Fish and Wildlife Area. Nothing extraordinary had taken place over the weekend. It had just been a few old friends gathered around the campfire reminiscing. That evening, however, they were casually snapping photos of each other when a strange light suddenly appeared in the western sky. One of the campers, John Kintz, quickly grabbed the camera and managed to capture the strange image on film.

Naturally the men were shocked and astonished. According to Kintz, the craft, which appeared to be cylindrical, hovered approximately 150 feet above the ground and maneuvered back and forth slowly and methodically. The object was elliptical in shape and had a large, protruding, circular dome on top that was surrounded by a ringlike formation.

The object was bright, but Kintz claims that it projected a

translucent light, which glowed with the luminosity of a bright moon. The saucer was completely silent. Kintz affirms that the entire time the object was in view it was completely noiseless and gave no indication of being propelled by any type of conventional powered engine. Kintz is a pilot and is particularly attuned to the sounds associated with most aircraft.

The Extraterrestrial Explanation Has Not Been Disproven

For most people, the term UFO is synonymous with extraterrestrial spacecraft. This is, of course, just one possible explanation for UFO phenomena. Until observation or theory make this explanation untenable, it should be considered a viable possibility.

No single explanation has provided a satisfying account of the entire UFO literature. Hoaxes, misperceptions, and misinterpretations explain specific cases. Yet some reports have not yielded to any prosaic explanation.

Stuart Appelle, *Mercury*, January/February 1995.

Before the craft departed, it moved lower and paused momentarily. The men noticed that the object became less bright and less translucent as it slowed down. The dome on top of the aircraft appeared very close and visible, and Kintz claims that he could almost see into the craft. It is important to note that the object did not seem to take a threatening stance, but rather moved about as if it were observing the men. Prior to departure, the saucer became more translucent, as if it were building up power. Suddenly, a red light flashed three times at the bottom of the craft, and in a matter of seconds it was gone. It had retreated as quickly as it had arrived.

Explanations?

As is the case with many UFO sightings, several other people reportedly saw the same object that night. The local newspaper received calls from people living in the surrounding area, but the reports were not taken seriously. No one at the local paper seemed to have any interest in following up on the unexplained sightings of that night. Interestingly enough, however, the La Grange Standard (the local newspaper) did run a short statement reporting that "several calls had been made to the paper reporting a UFO, but not to worry, because the object sighted was merely a blimp, which happened to be passing over the area."

Regardless of what skeptics and non-believers may say about

the possibilities of UFOs visiting and exploring our atmosphere, there are those who continue to have an open mind and remain objective about the possibility of alien intelligence. These individuals are to be commended for their objectivity and their ability to expand their intelligence to encompass new ideas.

To those non-believers who insist on concrete, rock-solid evidence in order to be persuaded, I can only say that science and unexplained phenomena are not always presented as factually and completely as we would like. It is up to us as intelligent human beings to take the knowledge we do have and piece it together in a sensible, factual format so we can try to understand what would otherwise remain an enigma.

| "No good physical evidence . . . supports the hypothesis that UFOs are extraterrestrial spacecraft."

UFOs ARE NOT EXTRATERRESTRIAL SPACECRAFT

Donald W. Goldsmith and Tobias C. Owen

Despite numerous reports of unidentified objects in the sky, Donald W. Goldsmith and Tobias C. Owen maintain in the following viewpoint that no physical evidence exists to suggest that UFOs are of extraterrestrial origin. They argue that because most UFOs can be explained as having natural causes, scientists should remain skeptical about the existence of alien spacecraft. Goldsmith, a science writer with Interstellar Media in Berkeley, California, cowrote the *Nova* television program "Is Anybody Out There?" Owen is a professor of astronomy at the University of Hawaii in Honolulu. They are the authors of *The Search for Life in the Universe.*

As you read, consider the following questions:

1. According to Goldsmith and Owen, what is the fourth point in the line of reasoning employed by proponents of the extraterrestrial hypothesis?
2. What examples do the authors give of claims that most people are normally skeptical about?
3. What are some of the natural causes that investigators have found for unidentified flying objects, according to the authors?

From Donald W. Goldsmith and Tobias C. Owen, "Should We Discount the Extraterrestrial Hypothesis for UFOs?" *Mercury* magazine, January/February 1995; ©1995 Astronomical Society of the Pacific. Reprinted with permission. This article was the affirmative answer to the above question posed in the Point/Counterpoint section of *Mercury* magazine and was opposed by another article answering in the negative.

No good physical evidence—photographic, spectroscopic, or other—supports the hypothesis that UFOs are extraterrestrial spacecraft. Without concrete evidence, the proponents of the ET hypothesis must use abstract reasoning. Theoretical analysis is not to be dismissed, but lacks credibility if it does not flow from reliable data and from physical laws on which nearly everyone can agree. Without experimental verification by independent investigators, gravitational waves, cold fusion, and alien spaceships all remain in the shadowy, if pleasing, domain of individual minds.

EXAMINING THE UFO HYPOTHESIS

The proponents of the ET hypothesis usually rely on the following line of argument:

- Our galaxy, let alone other galaxies, may harbor an enormous number of civilizations.
- Some of them may have the interest in and aptitude for interstellar space flight.
- Using their sophisticated technology, the civilizations that do visit can send as many spacecraft as they like and can perform whatever feats they choose.
- We cannot determine the natural cause of mysterious objects in the sky. Extraterrestrial visitors are the most likely explanation.

Many scientists agree with the first two points, even with the third: A scientific, technology-blind analysis suggests that interstellar flight requires a stupendous amount of energy, but we must allow for the possibility that other civilizations have discovered a deep secret we don't know. Therefore, we might be led to the conclusion that aliens are among us.

We are intrigued and excited by the fact that we don't know everything. But we insist on real evidence before we can accept the idea that visitors are flashing through our skies and abducting our citizens. Most people, for solid reasons, are equally skeptical about far less earthshaking claims. They want to be sure that a new car or TV will perform as advertised, and do not simply accept as valid the claims of others—especially claims made by people with financial or emotional interest in them. The careful consumer wants to do an experiment: take a test-drive, turn the set on for themselves.

Unfortunately the UFO data consist almost entirely of eyewitness accounts of things seen in the sky. Scientists in general are not accustomed to dealing with such data, which are notoriously difficult to interpret. Consider a famous event that had nothing to do with UFOs: the assassination of President John F. Kennedy in 1963. There were witnesses, testimony, photographs, various sound recordings, a film, all of which were thoroughly analyzed. Yet the events have been a source of seemingly endless dispute.

UFOs Are Not Extraterrestrial

UFO investigator Alvin Lawson is both believer and nonbeliever. He believes there are UFOs, but he doesn't believe that space aliens are flying them.

"Do I think there are unidentified flying objects, things that people can't explain what they are or why they're there? Yes," says Lawson, director of the Garden Grove–based UFO Reports Center of Orange County.

"Do I think that little green men are inside them abducting people? No."

John Woolard, *San Diego Union-Tribune*, September 16, 1996.

Now contrast that event with the average UFO report, where one or two people see something in the sky and later try to describe what they saw. This in itself does not make bad science. Eye-witness accounts helped the German physicist Chladni (1756–1827) to deduce the extraterrestrial origin of meteorites. But he had been trained as a lawyer before he studied physics and was well equipped to evaluate testimony. When serious investigators who have the necessary skills examine UFO reports, they invariably find some natural cause. Venus, meteors, falling space debris, clouds, migrating birds, airplanes, and even automobiles on elevated roadways have all been mistaken for alien space-craft, to say nothing of deliberate hoaxes.

UNIDENTIFIED BUT NOT EXTRATERRESTRIAL

As scientists, we must always keep our eyes open for new phenomena and our minds open to new hypotheses. Yet we insist that any hypothesis be tested before we accept it. We believe in the reality of the UFO phenomenon, because people certainly see things in the sky that they cannot identify. But experience has shown that what they see can be explained in terms of phenomena we already know.

| "The chance for intelligent life elsewhere in our universe is indeed good."

LIFE PROBABLY EXISTS ON OTHER PLANETS

Julie Paque

In the following viewpoint, Julie Paque examines different theories about how life originated on Earth. Some scientists maintain that life started through chemical processes here on the planet, she reports, while others believe that organic material was deposited on Earth from comets and other space debris. Either way, she argues, the fact that sentient life arose on Earth implies that intelligent life probably exists on at least one of the many billions of planets elsewhere in the universe. Paque is an associate research scientist at the SETI (Search for Extraterrestrial Intelligence) Institute in Moffett Field, California.

As you read, consider the following questions:

1. According to Paque, what two things were necessary for amino acids to form from methane, water, and ammonia?
2. How much organic material falls to Earth from space every year, in the author's estimate?
3. How many stars does the Milky Way galaxy contain, according to the author?

From Julie Paque, "What Makes a Planet a Friend for Life?" *Astronomy*, June 1995. Reprinted by permission of Kalmbach Publishing Co.

By all rights, Earth should be lifeless. As dead as a doornail. As dead, in fact, as the Moon, which it largely resembled four billion years ago.

How life began on Earth is at present a mystery, although scientists have made a bit of progress charting its first steps.

Life's beginnings can be traced back to primitive organic molecules that formed on Earth and learned how to copy themselves. How the organic stuff that made self-replicating molecules got on Earth, exactly how it combined, and what that process says about the existence of life elsewhere in the universe are still largely open questions. Many scientists believe the molecules arose in the soupy oceans of Earth, while others think they were deposited on Earth from space. Understanding which idea is correct will permit astronomers to better estimate the relative number of living planets, which they have already done in rough fashion using a formula called the Drake equation. It uses a number of variables about stars, planetary systems, and the chemistry of life to estimate the possible number of living planets in the universe.

It's ALIVE!

To search for life's origins astronomers must first define life. Living things are organisms as we know them on Earth, organisms based primarily on carbon but also on hydrogen, oxygen, and nitrogen. Imagination, with generous assistance from television dramas, suggests that other forms of life, perhaps based primarily on some element other than carbon, may exist elsewhere in the universe. But as yet scientists have no evidence to support the possibility of life based on other elements, so this discussion will focus on life as it exists on Earth.

Once upon a time humans considered the constituents of life to be the "elements" fire, water, air, and earth. Now of course scientists know the periodic table of the elements and have a detailed knowledge of organisms on the molecular and cellular level.

All living beings are composed of cells, and within each cell are proteins, which regulate carbohydrates and fats. Proteins in turn are composed of amino acids. The nucleic acids RNA (ribonucleic acid) and DNA (deoxyribonucleic acid) within the cells orchestrate how these amino acids link into proteins.

Besides being composed of cells, living beings share other characteristics. They metabolize energy from the environment (by eating), and they reproduce and pass along their genes to succeeding generations. Mutation, which introduces random changes in cells, is also a factor in the evolution of life, although only a moderate one. Such changes sometimes create stronger, more efficient individuals that compete more successfully for the available food and have a better chance of surviving to pass along their genes than average beings. Additionally, some living beings are sentient, meaning they have the power of perception by sense. Animals and plants share these traits.

THE COSMIC SEEDS OF LIFE

Until recently, science continued to ask how the nucleic and amino acids arose. They have long believed compounds as complex as amino acids formed from methane, water, and ammonia. To do this on early Earth, two other things were needed, an oxygen-poor environment (like that on early Earth) and energy such as lightning, volcanic eruptions, or simply the Sun's radiation. The amino acids then formed proteins and nucleic acids. DNA and RNA are the blueprints for proteins, but they also need proteins as catalysts. So molecular biologists have something of a chicken and egg problem. Which came first—proteins or nucleic acids? Current research leans towards the RNA-first solution.

Whichever chemicals battled their way out of the soup first, life's stage was set as long as four billion years ago, when the number of objects impacting onto our planet started to slow down. Periodic impacts of large comets and asteroids undoubtedly changed the variety and quantity of organic material available to make more complex molecules. The first fossil evidence of life contains bacteria-like beings entombed in rocks about 3.5 billion years old.

In 1953, chemists Stanley L. Miller and Harold C. Urey produced amino acids in a laboratory from methane, ammonia, water, and hydrogen. If Miller and Urey had left this simple brew of chemicals on a lab bench, in a freezer, or in a warm bowl, nothing would have happened. Instead, they carefully recreated an oxygen-poor atmosphere like that of the early Earth by adding excess hydrogen, methane, carbon monoxide, and ammonia, and sparked the mixture with energy to simulate that contributed by the lightning common on early Earth. These classic experiments showed that the chemicals and conditions on early Earth could have produced amino acids in a very short time.

Since the Miller-Urey experiment, scientists have investigated where such chemical activity might have occurred on early Earth. Two locales may have acted as the mixing bowl: Earth's atmosphere or its oceans. The viability of each area depends on the nature of Earth's early atmosphere, and scientists hold a range of opinions on that. Many believe it was highly reducing, or oxygen poor, while others disagree. Compounds important in forming life, like formaldehyde and hydrogen cyanide, are easiest to produce experimentally under oxygen-poor conditions. Earth's early ocean was almost certainly oxygen-poor, illustrated by Precambrian banded iron formations that precipitated from early seas. If the early atmosphere didn't, the early oceans almost certainly provided a habitat where organic molecules could combine into amino acids.

There's another possibility. Sherwood Chang, a planetary biologist at NASA Ames Research Center, points out that the ocean surface could have been a favorable setting. A complex set of physical and chemical processes operate here. Gases, aerosols, and dust from the atmosphere were continually mixed by wind and waves with the contents of the early ocean. Compounds were able to exist in gas, liquid, and solid states and ideal conditions existed for organic molecules to form.

So the first amino acids and proteins may have formed above the ocean or at the meeting place of ocean and volcano, which would have provided energy as well, and spread from there. Anyone who has seen dramatic images of an undersea vent or volcano splattering lava into the ocean can appreciate the unusual conditions. Life may have taken a foothold around a "black smoker" pouring energy out deep within the ocean.

Other locales may have existed, too. Verne Oberbeck, also at Ames, has proposed that raindrops may have hosted organic chemical reactions on early Earth.

ORGANIC STUFF FROM SPACE

On the other hand, comets and asteroids dumped a great amount of material onto early Earth. Anyone who followed the 1994 impact of Comet Shoemaker-Levy 9 into Jupiter can appreciate how a comet could dump material onto a planet. Several billion years ago vastly more such objects were orbiting and impacting bodies in the inner solar system. Analysis of Comet Halley indicates that approximately one-third of its mass consists of organic molecules. If Halley is like other comets, then, comets contain substantial amounts of organic molecules.

Organics may have come from asteroids striking Earth, too. Carbonaceous chondrites, as their name implies, contain carbon and as much as 5 percent organic matter. The carbonaceous chondrite called Murchison, which fell in Australia in 1969, contains a variety of amino acids. Astronomers believe, then, that in some cases organic molecules from an asteroid or comet have survived the incredible crushing pressures and superhot temperatures of a planetary strike.

Not all of the organic material that struck Earth hit with the dramatic force of asteroids and comets, however. Just as significantly, a continuous silent rain of interplanetary dust particles falls slowly to Earth even today. These particles are microscopic, highly porous aggregates of mineral and organic material thought to have originated in comets and asteroids. Their carbon content can be as high as 40 percent. Three hundred tons of this stuff falls gracefully to Earth every year, gently depositing particles in our backyards and offices and on our houses and cars.

ASTRONOMERS AGREE: THERE IS LIFE IN OUTER SPACE

The universe is vast beyond comprehension. A half-trillion stars patiently wheel in the slow dance of the Milky Way galaxy. So great is their number that they meld into a continuous band of light across the nighttime sky, despite the fact that each is separated from its neighbors by tens of trillions of miles. Beyond the Milky Way, the frozen vacuum of space is interrupted by the glow of other galaxies, each with its own prodigious complement of stars: It is a pattern that repeats as far as we can see, to the dim, red limits of the measurable universe.

In all this enormity, Earth appears to be of the smallest consequence: a tiny plankton in an immense sea, and neither special nor remarkable. It is not surprising, then, that if you ask a roomful of astronomers whether they believe that life exists elsewhere, whether there might be other plankton afloat in the cosmic sea, their response is overwhelmingly affirmative.

Seth Shostak, *World & I*, June 1995.

Some planetary scientists approach the extraterrestrial delivery of organics more creatively. Ted Bunch of NASA's Ames Research Center and Jeff Bada and Luann Becker of the Scripps Institution of Oceanography have found fullerenes in the Sudbury impact crater in Ontario, Canada. These organic compounds, also called buckyballs, probably formed during the Sudbury impact from carbonlike compounds in the impacting body. Bunch and his colleagues are now experimentally testing the survivability of organic material that could remain viable on Earth or create new compounds like buckyballs in an impact. Early test results are encouraging: Bunch's group has found that complex organics called polycyclic aromatic hydrocarbons are created during the impact of a carbonaceous chondrite into aluminum at velocities of up to 6.5 kilometers per second.

Survival of organics on a comet or asteroid remains an open question. In 1992 Christopher Chyba and his colleagues at Cornell University estimated the survivability of organic material as it passes through the atmosphere and impacts Earth. Large asteroids vaporize rock and water, destroying organic material, and generally devastate the environment. The large impact that produced the Chicxulub Crater on the Yucatan peninsula wiped out the dinosaurs. Such events were likely more common earlier in Earth's history and probably more devastating to the limited range of life forms present then. If Earth's early atmosphere had been denser, comets could have been slowed enough during entry for organic material to survive. Chyba's research shows that smaller, less dense asteroids or comets probably could contribute organic material to Earth, and certainly interplanetary dust particles could.

Even if asteroids and comets delivered life's building blocks, the terrific power of volcanoes, along with the ongoing bombardment, may have snuffed out life many times in its infancy. Early Earth was a rather inhospitable place. That's fortunate for humans, though. Life might be very different if one of the earlier attempts had taken. Wouldn't it be ironic if a comet carried the building blocks of life and another comet wiped out the dinosaurs? Perhaps a comet will strike Earth again, rendering humans extinct, and leaving the planet open for a third master species—maybe ferrets or 13-lined ground squirrels.

IS ANYBODY HOME?

Whether or not comets or asteroids helped life arise on Earth, our home planet and its inhabitants imply that life might be common on other planets in the Milky Way Galaxy and in other galaxies scattered across the universe. Frank Drake, president of the SETI (Search for Extraterrestrial Intelligence) Institute, has devised an equation to estimate the likelihood that technological civilizations exist in the universe (N):

$$N = R^* \cdot f_p \cdot n_e \cdot f_l \cdot f_i{}^a f_c \cdot L.$$

R^* is the rate of formation of stars suitable for development of intelligent life, and f_p is the fraction of stars with planetary systems. Of the planets in a planetary system, only a certain proportion have the environmental conditions necessary to sustain life (n_e), and only some of those planets will actually have life (f_l). Intelligent life will emerge on only a fraction of the planets (f_i) that contain life of any sort, and only some will be technologically advanced enough for their existence to be detectable from space (f_c). The factor L in the Drake equation reflects the length of time detectable signals are released into space. If all global lifespans of technological species survive only thousands of years our chance of detecting them is lower than if they survive for millions of years.

Placing conservative estimates for each of these factors into the equation leads to the conclusion that the chance for intelligent life elsewhere in our universe is indeed good. The chance that life of any sort exists elsewhere is even better. Astronomers know the physical laws and chemistry of the universe hold constant everywhere astronomers observe them, even in the hearts of quasars in the early days of the universe some 15 billion years ago. Our Milky Way Galaxy contains as many as 400 billion stars. Astronomers estimate that at least 100 billion galaxies exist. You figure it out: Even with ridiculously conservative estimates, the potential number of stars with planets that have life is astonishingly high. That does not mean that astronomers can find life with ease, however.

DETECTING OTHER PLANETS

Living on the only planet known to harbor life, astronomers have thus far concentrated their efforts on identifying star systems with Earth-like planets. Several problems complicate searches for planetary systems around other stars, mainly the difficulty in resolving a small, distant dark object near a star that is orders of magnitude brighter. Rather than observing in optical light, however, astronomers can observe in the infrared part of the spectrum to decrease this contrast, or they can indirectly detect planetary systems by measuring the gentle wobble in a star's path across the sky caused by the mass of orbiting planets.

Currently forming planetary systems are easier to observe, as the disks of gas and dust that surround their young suns absorb and emit lots more radiation than planets do.

A planet that supports carbon-based life such as ours must also have liquid water, and this considerably restricts the range of temperatures on the planet and requires an atmosphere so the water won't escape into space. Many other factors make life possible for humanlike beings, including visible light, gravity, a breathable atmosphere of oxygen and water vapor, and the right range of temperatures.

Beginning to comprehend how life on Earth rose out of a cosmic stew of organic molecules certainly gives us fresh respect for our fragile planet. Knowing what makes Earth habitable will help humans maintain their home and perhaps one day in the distant future allow our descendants to leave the planet, when our Sun ages, to find shelter among the stars. Perhaps in the interim humans will discover sentient life in the universe and come to learn the perspective of this life on our own civilization. If astronomers do discover the range of life that probably exists out there, it will certainly bring human beings a little closer in our common journey through space and time.

"There is no observational evidence whatsoever for the existence of other intelligent beings anywhere in the universe."

LIFE PROBABLY DOES NOT EXIST ON OTHER PLANETS

Robert Naeye

In January 1996, astronomers discovered planets orbiting distant stars, which they maintained might be inhabited by extraterrestrial life. In the following viewpoint, however, Robert Naeye argues that it is very improbable that intelligent life exists elsewhere in the universe. There are very specific conditions necessary for simple living organisms to exist on this planet, he maintains, and these conditions are not likely to exist elsewhere. Further, Naeye asserts, it is even more unlikely that intelligent life has evolved anywhere but Earth. Naeye is an associate editor of *Astronomy* magazine.

As you read, consider the following questions:

1. In Naeye's opinion, why does intelligent life need to be based on liquid water, as opposed to some other liquid?
2. According to the author, why is the 47 Ursae Majoris system not a good candidate for life?
3. According to Ernst Mayr, cited by the author, how many years of evolution were necessary to produce intelligent life?

From Robert Naeye, "OK, Where Are They?" *Astronomy*, July 1996. Reprinted by permission of Kalmbach Publishing Co.

Humans thrive nearly everywhere on Earth. From the sweltering Amazon rain forest to the bone-dry Sahara Desert, and from the frigid Arctic wastelands to isolated Pacific islands, people have adapted to hostile conditions.

Is the Milky Way Galaxy like planet Earth, with towns and cities dotting the landscape? Or is Earth more like a lonely island in a vast galactic ocean, with life-bearing planets and especially intelligent life separated by vast distances?

On the surface, the most obvious evidence bearing on these questions is the fact that our home world and host star seem so ordinary. Nicolas Copernicus shattered the prevailing notion that Earth was seated at the center of creation. Succeeding generations of astronomers steadily reinforced the Copernican view as they discovered the true nature of stars, the remote location of our home world within our Galaxy, and the existence of galaxies far, far beyond our own. So pervasive is this view that in the world of modern science, it is almost considered heresy to assert any special qualities to our solar system, our planet, or even ourselves. With an estimated 200 billion stars in the Galaxy and interstellar space filled with the molecules necessary for life, many scientists and laymen naturally conclude that we could not be alone—we must share our Galaxy with hundreds, thousands, or perhaps millions of other civilizations.

THE CHANCES OF LIFE ARE ONE IN A MILLION

But on closer examination, this simple logic falls apart. Recent studies in a variety of scientific fields suggest that life must pass through a series of bottlenecks on the road to intelligence. On Earth, a long sequence of improbable events transpired in just the right way to bring forth our existence, as if we had won a million-dollar lottery a million times in a row. Contrary to the prevailing belief, maybe we are special. Maybe humanity stands alone on a fertile island in the largely sterile waters of the galactic ocean.

Scientists who ponder this deep question are limited by the fact they have only one example of life to study: life on Earth. Science-fiction writers have envisioned an amazing variety of life-forms totally unlike any on our planet. But sci-fi writers are limited only by their imaginations, not by physical reality. Life as we know it, from astronomy aficionados to the lowest bacteria, shares several fundamental characteristics, and most scientists think these will be common to all life in the universe.

First, life takes in matter and energy from its surroundings, uses it for food, reproduction, and locomotion, and expels waste. Second, life stores information and replicates it in future generations (that's a fancy way of saying "sex").

The liquid state is ideal for these tasks. Liquids can dissolve both solids and gases, producing complex molecules. And those molecules can move about freely and come into contact with other molecules, hastening chemical reactions. In gases, atoms lie too far apart to allow the formation of complex molecules capable of storing information. And in solids, molecules are locked in place, so chemical reactions necessary to transfer information from generation to generation proceed much more slowly than in liquids. On Earth, where all life is based on the liquid state, 3.8 billion years elapsed between the first microbes and fast food restaurants. If life on another planet were based on solids, the time needed for intelligent life to evolve would be longer than the age of the universe.

Intelligent life not only needs to be based on a liquid, it probably needs to be based on liquid water. On Earth, water is literally the molecule of life, comprising 70 percent of a cell's mass. There are good reasons to think this will be true elsewhere. Water is the most abundant molecule in the universe likely to be found in a liquid state and it has a wonderful ability to dissolve inorganic chemicals so living organisms can use them. Other liquids, such as ammonia, don't share water's versatility. It's no coincidence that the only body in the solar system with liquid water on its surface—Earth—is the only known life-bearing world.

Some life-forms in the universe might be based on other liquids, but most biologists think the ones most likely to evolve high intelligence will be based on water. This establishes a rather stringent requirement for intelligent life: It needs a stable temperature for billions of years so water can remain in a liquid state.

EARTH'S SPECIAL SUN

To evolve intelligence, life needs a star that can serve as an incubator for a life-bearing planet by providing relatively stable temperatures for billions of years. But only a small fraction of the Milky Way Galaxy's 200 billion stars fit the bill.

One that fits it perfectly is the Sun. This middle-aged star has a slightly above-average size and mass, and it produces a steady energy output. But the Sun, unlike the majority of stars, has no stellar companion. Roughly two-thirds of Milky Way stars belong to binary or multiple star systems. In most multiple star systems, either planets won't form, or varying gravitational forces will yank planets into tortured, elongated orbits. At one point in its orbit a planet will come very close to a star's searing heat, causing liquid water to evaporate. At other times it will venture far, far away, and water will freeze as temperatures plunge to a few degrees above absolute zero. Intelligent life could never evolve on such planets.

Most single stars cannot support life either. Some 80 percent of all stars—those with less than 65 percent of the Sun's mass—are just too wimpy to support life because they radiate so little energy. A planet close enough to receive enough heat to keep water in a liquid state will orbit so close that tidal forces from the star will slow the planet's rotation to a crawl, as happens between Mercury and the Sun. One hemisphere faces the star for extended periods of time, becoming too hot, and the other faces away, becoming too cold. Many of these dwarf stars also spew huge flares into space that periodically toast any nearby planets.

The Conditions Necessary for Life

There are evidently rather narrow constraints for the possibility of the origin and maintenance of life on a planet. There has to be a favorable average temperature; the seasonal variation should not be too extreme; the planet must have a suitable distance from its sun; it must have the appropriate mass so that its gravity can hold an atmosphere; this atmosphere must have the right chemical composition to support early life; it must have the necessary consistency to protect the new life against ultraviolet and other harmful radiations; and there must be water on such a planet. In other words, all environmental conditions must be suitable for the origin and maintenance of life.

Ernst Mayr, *Planetary Report*, May/June 1996.

On the other end of the scale, stars 40 percent more massive than the Sun or larger don't live long enough to produce technological civilizations. These celestial behemoths, which make up about one percent of the Galaxy's total, consume their hydrogen fuel like hungry sharks at a feeding frenzy. On the cosmic time scale, they live out their lives in a blink of an eye.

The Sun belongs to a precious minority of stars that have no stellar companions and that have the right mass. Nobody knows exactly how many stars can support intelligent life, but it's clear these criteria have put a dent in the most optimistic ET claims by whittling 200 billion stars down to perhaps 10 to 20 billion.

Ten or 20 billion good suns is still a lot of good suns. But how many have planets that can support life? The discovery in

January 1996 of planets orbiting the Sun-like stars 51 Pegasi, 70 Virginis, and 47 Ursae Majoris has fueled the optimism of extraterrestrial life proponents. But on closer inspection, the new planets paint a less rosy picture.

The planet orbiting 51 Pegasi is a Jupiter-mass world orbiting so close to its star that it's baked to a searing 1000 degrees. Most astronomers think the planet formed much farther from its star and then migrated inward due to tidal interactions with the disk from which the planet formed, stopping just short of a fiery death. But if the system once contained terrestrial planets, they weren't so lucky. Astronomers think terrestrial planets will spiral into their parent star—and their doom—if the protoplanetary disk is long-lived.

The 70 Virginis planet has been touted as a good life-bearing candidate because it lies in a zone where water can exist in liquid form. But the planet has a highly elliptical orbit, subjecting the world (and any moons that might be orbiting it) to wild climate variations. Moreover, the planet is so massive (at least 6.5 times that of Jupiter) that its elliptical orbit would completely eject any inner planets from the system.

Of all the new planetary systems discovered to date, the 47 Ursae Majoris system is the closest analog to our own. But even that system offers little prospect for life. Most astronomers think Jupiter's immense gravity prevented a planet from forming in the asteroid belt. The 47 Ursae Majoris planet, being at least 2.3 times more massive than Jupiter and closer to its star, would play havoc with the planet-formation process within the star's life zone.

JUPITER'S ROLE IN PROTECTING EARTH

Astronomers have good reason to think that planetary systems like our own—with rocky inner planets and gas giants starting at about Jupiter's distance from the Sun—offer the best prospects for life. The rocky planets serve as the abodes for life, while the massive planets cleanse the systems of most of the junk left over from the planet-formation process. Computer simulations by George Wetherill of the Carnegie Institution in Washington, D.C., show that without Jupiters, killer asteroids and comets would constantly bombard any rocky inner planets. Instead of impact-induced mass extinctions (like the one that wiped out the dinosaurs) occurring every 100 million years, they would happen every 100,000 years. Life would never have the opportunity to evolve toward intelligence.

But astronomers have unsuccessfully searched several dozen nearby Sun-like stars for Jupiter-mass planets in Jupiter-like orbits, suggesting that gas giant planets might be relatively uncommon. Computer models indicate that a planet needs at least 10 million years to gobble up enough gas from a protoplanetary disk to attain the mass of Jupiter. Radio observations of nearby stars only a few million years old show that most are not surrounded by enough gas to form heavyweight planets like Jupiter. So for a solar system to be habitable, it needs to form from a disk that lives long enough to enable a Jupiter to rein in sufficient gas, but not so long that the terrestrial planets spiral all the way into the star. Our solar system might be one of the few where everything happened just right to give life a fighting chance. . . .

EARTH'S THERMOSTAT

But perhaps the most fortuitous circumstance of all is the fact that water remained in a liquid state as the Earth and Sun went through major changes. When Earth formed 4.6 billion years ago, the Sun was 30 percent dimmer than it is now, according to stellar evolution models. At the time, Earth had a totally different atmosphere. It started off with an atmosphere consisting mostly of nitrogen, carbon dioxide, and carbon monoxide. Over billions of years, biological and geological activity removed most of the carbon from the atmosphere and replaced it with the free oxygen that now provides sustenance for all animal life.

Remarkably, as the Sun heated up, and Earth's atmosphere completely changed over in composition, Earth's average temperature remained confined within a narrow range conducive to life, always staying between 5 and 60 degrees Celsius. How has Earth managed to avoid either a runaway greenhouse effect or a permanent ice age?

Geologists propose that a global thermostat ensures the atmosphere becomes neither too hot nor too cold. Volcanism and the motions of shifting oceanic and continental plates cycle carbon between the atmosphere and the interior. When Earth's climate cools, the process allows carbon dioxide levels in the atmosphere to rise. Since carbon dioxide is a greenhouse gas that traps heat, this warms the planet. When the Earth warms up, the mechanism removes carbon dioxide from the atmosphere, so the planet cools. This thermostat, many Earth scientists believe, has maintained a stable climate for eons.

How many planetary systems in the Galaxy orbit a good sun, have a Jupiter, and have a rocky planet . . . a perfectly working thermostat? No one can say for sure, but it's probably a very small number. The moral of the story is that good planets are hard to find.

Even if we assume that life originates on a good planet orbiting a good sun, it's by no means inevitable that a species with high intelligence will ever evolve. Many evolutionary biologists think the evolution of a highly intelligent species like *Homo sapiens* was a one-in-a-billion long shot.

In his book *Wonderful Life*, Harvard paleontologist Stephen Jay Gould corrects the common misconception that evolution is a "march of progress" toward increasingly advanced life and intelligence. Instead, as Gould explains, the evolution of life is like a tree. *Homo sapiens*, like all of Earth's modern-day species, is but one tiny twig at the end of a long chain of increasingly smaller branches. No single twig is more "advanced" than any other twig; evolution does not work toward a goal.

Gould's Harvard colleague Ernst Mayr argues that the evolution of a twig capable of high technology is exceedingly improbable. He notes that only one of the four major kingdoms of life, the animals, went on to produce intelligence. Only one of the 70 phyla of animals, the chordates, produced intelligence. Only one class of chordates, the mammals, produced intelligence. Only one order of mammals, the primates, and only one family of primates, the great apes, produced high intelligence. And only after 25 million years of evolution and many failed lineages, did one particular ape evolve that was capable of high technology.

Our own lineage went through millions of species. Because evolution is primarily a game of chance, any seemingly minor past event could have gone slightly different, cutting off our evolutionary line before humans evolved. ET proponents should be deeply discouraged that none of the millions of other lineages, representing the billions of species that have inhabited Earth during its existence, have made substantial progress toward high intelligence.

Unlike the development of eyes, which have evolved independently at least 40 different times in Earth's history, there has been no evolutionary "convergence" toward high intelligence. Intelligence may have evolved several times, but only in humans was it combined with the manual dexterity needed to make tools. And that combination seems to be the key that allowed humans to develop their high technology.

WHERE ARE THE ALIENS?

The long series of bottlenecks makes it clear that the emergence of intelligent life is far more difficult than scientists once thought. There are probably more obstacles that scientists haven't even stumbled across yet. The origin of life on Earth, for example, might have been the ultimate long shot. ET proponents might counter that this line of reasoning is based on mere anthropocentric speculation. Maybe life and even intelligent life can take on various forms that we can't even imagine.

But alternative life-forms are the epitome of speculation. If one chooses to shun speculation and stick solely with observations, one can ask the same question that Nobel physicist Enrico Fermi put forth in 1950: If the Galaxy is teeming with intelligent life, where are they? The sobering reality is that there is no observational evidence whatsoever for the existence of other intelligent beings anywhere in the universe.

"*After working with 20 or so abductees, . . . it became clear to me that I was dealing with a phenomenon that could not be explained psychiatrically.*"

HUMANS ARE BEING ABDUCTED BY ALIENS

John E. Mack

A number of ordinary, sane people have reported being abducted by extraterrestrial aliens, taken aboard spaceships, and subjected to biological examinations and experiments. John E. Mack, a psychiatrist who has interviewed some of these abductees, believes that the abduction accounts are true. In the following viewpoint, he maintains that physical evidence and similarities between abductees' accounts support the validity of these stories. Mack is a professor of psychiatry at Cambridge Hospital, Harvard Medical School. He is the author of *Abduction: Human Encounters with Aliens*, from which this viewpoint is adapted.

As you read, consider the following questions:

1. In Mack's opinion, how might the abduction phenomenon affect the way humans see themselves?
2. What are the several types of aliens described by Mack?
3. What is the "ontological shock" that abductees experience, according to the author?

I feel sometimes that in the mental health profession we are like the generals who are accused of always fighting the last war, invoking the diagnoses and mental mechanisms with which we are familiar when confronted with a new and mysterious phenomenon, especially if it is one that challenges our way of thinking.

Thus, when I first heard of a man named Budd Hopkins who worked with people who reported being taken into spaceships, I said something to the effect that he must be crazy and so must they. Nothing in my then nearly 40 years of familiarity with the field of psychiatry prepared me for what I came to learn.

After working with 20 or so abductees between 1990 and 1994, it became clear to me that I was dealing with a phenomenon that could not be explained psychiatrically, yet was simply *not possible* within the framework of the Western scientific worldview.

My choices then were these: either to stretch psychology beyond reasonable limits, overlooking aspects of the phenomenon that could not be explained psychologically, or to open to the possibility that our consensus framework of reality is too limited. Perhaps a phenomenon such as this cannot be explained within its ontological parameters.

For a clinician like myself, trained in the Western tradition, the temptation is to accept some experiences and reject others as too "far out." I suspect such discriminations are not wise or useful. My criterion for including or crediting an observation by an abductee is simply whether what has been reported was felt to be real by the experiencer and was communicated sincerely and authentically to me.

ABDUCTEES ARE NORMAL PEOPLE

I do know that none of the efforts to characterize the abductees as a group has been successful. Abductees seem to come, as if at random, from all parts of society. My own sample includes students, housewives, secretaries, writers, business people, computer industry professionals, musicians, psychologists, a nightclub receptionist, a prison guard, an acupuncturist, a social worker and a gas station attendant.

At first I thought that working-class people predominated, but that appears to be related to the fact that those with less of an economic and social stake in the society seem less reluctant to come forward. Conversely, more professionally prominent abductees fear the threat to their position that public revelation of their experiences might bring. One of the men with whom I have worked did not tell me his real name until some trust had been established between us.

Psychological testing of abductees has not revealed evidence of mental or emotional disturbance that could account for these reports. My own sample demonstrates a broad range of mental health and emotional adaptation. Some experiencers are highly functioning individuals. Others verge on being overwhelmed by the traumatic impact and philosophical implications of their experiences.

I now feel that the phenomenon has potentially important implications for how we see ourselves in a larger sense, for it seems to shatter the notion that we are the preeminent intelligence in the cosmos, masters of our fate.

ANATOMY OF AN ABDUCTION

Abduction encounters begin most commonly in homes or when abductees are driving automobiles. In some cases the experiencer may be walking in nature. One woman was taken from a snowmobile on a winter's day. Children have experienced being taken from schoolyards. The first indication that an abduction is about to occur might be an unexplained intense blue or white light that floods the bedroom, an odd buzzing or humming sound, unexplained apprehension, the sense of an unusual presence or even the direct sighting of one or more humanoid beings in the room, and, of course, the close-up sighting of a strange craft.

When an abduction begins during the night or, as is common, during the early hours of the morning, the experiencer may at first call what is happening a dream. But careful questioning will reveal that the experiencer had not fallen asleep at all, or that the experience began in a conscious state after awakening.

After the initial contact, abductees are "floated" (the word most commonly used) down the hall, through the wall or windows of the house, or through the roof of the car. They are usually astounded to discover that they are passed through solid objects, experiencing only a slight vibratory sensation. In most cases the beam of light seems to serve as an energy source or "ramp" for transporting the abductee from the place where the abduction starts to a waiting vehicle.

After they are taken from the house, abductees often see a small spacecraft that may be standing on long legs. They are initially taken into this craft, which then rises to a second larger or "mother" ship. At other times they experience being taken up through the night sky directly to the large ship and will see the house or ground below receding dramatically. Often the abductee will struggle at this and later points to stop the experience, but this does little good except to give the individual a vital sense that he or she is not simply a passive victim.

DESCRIPTIONS OF ALIENS

Inside the ships, the abductees usually witness more alien beings, who are busy doing various tasks related to monitoring the equipment and handling the abduction procedures. The beings described by my cases are of several sorts. They appear as luminous entities that may be translucent, or at least not altogether solid. Reptilian creatures have been seen that seem to be carrying out mechanical functions. But by far the most common entity observed are the small "grays," humanoid beings three to four feet in height.

The grays are mainly of two kinds—smaller drone or insect-like workers, who move or glide robotically outside and inside the ships and perform various specific tasks, and a slightly taller leader or "doctor," as the abductees most often call him. Female "nurses," or other beings with special functions, are observed. The leader is usually felt to be male, although female leaders are also seen. Gender difference is not determined so much anatomically as by an intuitive feeling that abductees find difficult to put into words.

The small grays have large, pear-shaped heads that protrude in the back, long arms with three or four long fingers, a thin torso and spindly legs. Feet are not often seen directly, and are usually covered with single-piece boots. The beings are hairless with no ears, have rudimentary nostril holes and a thin slit for a mouth that rarely opens or is expressive of emotion. By far the most prominent features are huge, black eyes that curve upward and are more rounded toward the center of the head and pointed at the outer edge. The eyes have a compelling power, and the abductees will often wish to avoid looking directly into them because of the overwhelming dread of their own sense of self, or loss of will, that occurs when they do so.

BIOLOGICAL EXPERIMENTS AND IMPLANTS

The procedures that occur on these ships have been described in great detail in the literature on abductions. The abductee is usually undressed and is forced onto a body-fitting table. Skin and hair and other samples from inside the body are taken with use of various instruments that the abductees can sometimes describe in great detail.

Instruments are used to penetrate virtually every part of the abductees' bodies, including the nose, sinuses, eyes, ears and other parts of the head, arms, legs, feet, abdomen, genitalia and more rarely the chest. The most common and evidently most important procedures involve the reproductive systems. Abductees experience being impregnated by the alien beings and later having an alien-human or human-human pregnancy removed. They see the little fetuses being put into containers on the ships, and during subsequent abductions may see incubators where the hybrid babies are being raised. Experiencers may also see older hybrid children, which they are told by the aliens, or know intuitively, are their own.

ABDUCTIONS CANNOT BE EXPLAINED PSYCHIATRICALLY

"I really knew when I first talked with them [UFO abductees] that this was something that I could not explain psychiatrically," John Mack says of his patients. . . . "It didn't sound like it behaved like anything that had a psychiatric origin. It behaved like a trauma." And traumas come from *outside*. Mack, the author of the classic *Nightmares and Human Conflicts*, also was convinced these stories weren't dreams: They had a narrative consistency, within themselves and from person to person. He was sure his abductees were not making up stories to get attention. "They don't *want* to believe it! It's the *last* thing they want! They want to be told that this is a dream, that this is even madness."

Stephen Rae, *New York Times Magazine*, March 20, 1994.

In sum, the purely biological aspect of the abduction phenomenon seems to have to do with a kind of genetic or quasi-genetic engineering for the purpose of creating human/alien hybrid offspring.

Abductees frequently report that some sort of homing object has been inserted in their bodies, so that aliens can track or monitor them. These so-called implants may be felt as small nodules below the skin, and in several cases tiny objects have been recovered and analyzed biochemically and electromicroscopically. Massachusetts Institute of Technology (MIT) physicist David Pritchard, who has also been analyzing an implant that came out of a man's penis, has written about the criteria for examining and determining the nature of such objects. I have myself studied a ½- to ¾-inch thin, wiry object that was given to me by one of my clients, a 24-year-old woman, after it came out of her nose following an abduction experience. Elemental analysis and electronic microscopic photography revealed an interestingly twisted fiber consisting of carbon, silicon, oxygen, no nitrogen, and traces of other elements. A carbon isotopic analysis was not remarkable. A nuclear biologist colleague said the "specimen" was not a naturally occurring biological subject but could be a manufactured fiber of some sort. It seemed difficult to know how to proceed further.

PSYCHOLOGICAL EFFECTS ON ABDUCTEES

Needless to say, abductions profoundly affect the lives of those who experience them. For example, abductees experience a lifelong sense of isolation and estrangement from those around them. One savvy 8-year-old abductee looked at me incredulously when I asked him if he told his friends about his "encounters," which he was able to distinguish sharply from dreams, even when they had to do with UFOs. "No, I don't tell anybody that I don't know that well," he said. "I just don't want them to know that I have encounters. I think that a lot of people I know get scared if they hear scary stories. . . . I guess people are like, 'Hey! That's too weird!'" As adults, abductees learn not to talk about their experiences, except under trusting circumstances.

Abductees also experience what I have called "ontological shock" as the reality of their encounters sinks in. They, like all of us, have been raised in the belief that we on Earth are largely alone in the universe and that it would simply not be possible for intelligent beings to enter our world without using a highly advanced form of our technology and obeying the laws of our physics. Abductees tend to persist in the hope that a psychological explanation for their experiences will be found.

The result of all these experiences for abductees is the discovery of a new and altered sense of their place in the cosmic design, one that is more modest, respectful and harmonious in relation to Earth and its living systems. A heightened sense of the sacredness of the natural world is experienced along with deep sadness about the apparent hopelessness of Earth's environmental crisis.

In that way, the abduction phenomenon seems to offer new perspectives on human destructiveness. The aliens, for example, seem genuinely puzzled about the extent of our aggressiveness toward one another and especially our apparent willingness to destroy the planet's life. As one abductee, Paul, told me when speaking from an alien point of view, "We don't understand why you choose destruction." Another abductee, Ed, says he was told of the "heavily destructive" path we were taking, which was also destructive to the "humanoid's planet."

GATHERING SCIENTIFIC PROOF OF ABDUCTIONS

In physics, psychology and other fields, the data we obtain is a function of the way we have gone about the task of gaining information. The empirical methods of Western science rely primarily on the physical senses and rational intellect for gaining knowledge, and were developed in part to avoid the subjectivity, contamination and sheer *messiness* of human emotion.

Yet the cost of this restricted way of knowing may be that we now learn about the physical world with only limited use of our faculties. In order to learn about the worlds "beyond the veil," as abductees put it, we may need a different kind of consciousness. This means that the process of gaining information about abductions is, to a large degree, "co-creative"—understanding comes to those who will accept it, and what I help bring forth from experiencers is something I am helping them to discover within themselves. But this co-creative aspect does not mean, as my critics sometimes have said, that I impose beliefs of my own about the phenomenon upon the experiencers, or even that I believe literally everything an abductee says.

I must stress that we do not know the source from which the UFOs or the alien beings come (whether or not, for example, they originate in the physical universe as modern astrophysics has described it). But they manifest in the physical world and bring about definable consequences in that domain. In virtually every case there are one or more concrete physical findings that accompany or follow the abduction experience, such as UFO sightings, burned earth where UFOs have landed and independent corroboration that the abductee's whereabouts are unknown at the time of the event.

Budd Hopkins has documented a case, now being widely discussed, where a woman made an unsolicited report to him that from the Brooklyn Bridge she saw one of his clients being taken by alien beings from her 12th-floor East River apartment into a waiting spacecraft that then plunged into the river below. These observations corresponded precisely with what the client had told Hopkins happened to her when he recovered her memories of an abduction that occurred in November 1989.

Sometimes, according to reports, the abductee may be noted to be missing for a half hour or more or, in rare cases, for days. But in these instances no one has seen him being taken into a spacecraft, and there is no firm proof that abduction was the cause of their absence.

THE MEANING OF ABDUCTIONS

Quite a few abductees have spoken to me of their sense that at least some of their experiences are not occurring within the physical space/time dimensions of the universe as we comprehend it. They speak of aliens breaking through from another dimension. Abductees, some of whom have little education to prepare them to explain about such abstractions or odd dislocations, will speak of the collapse of space/time.

Those investigators who perceive the UFO abduction phenomenon from an adversarial perspective tend to interpret its meaning one-sidedly. The aliens are using us, the argument goes, for their own purposes, replenishing their genetic stock at our expense after some sort of holocaust on their own planet. I would not say that the aliens never resort to deception to hide their purposes, but the above argument is, in my view, too narrow or linear an interpretation.

My own impression is that we may be witnessing something far more complex, namely an awkward joining of two species, engineered by an intelligence we are unable to fathom, for a purpose that serves both of our goals with difficulties for each. I base this view on the evidence presented by the abductees themselves.

Many abduction experiences are unequivocally spiritual, which usually involves some sort of powerful encounter with, or immersion in, divine light. A number of abductees with whom I have worked experience at certain points an opening up to the source of being in the cosmos, which they often call Home, and from which they feel they have been brutally cut off in the course of becoming embodied as a human being. They may weep ecstatically when during our sessions they experience an opening or return to Home. They may rather resent having to remain on Earth in embodied form, even as they realize that on Earth they have some sort of mission to assist in bringing about a change in human consciousness.

| "Alien abductions may just be a modern equivalent of a sleep paralysis myth."

HUMANS ARE NOT BEING ABDUCTED BY ALIENS

Susan Blackmore

In the following viewpoint, Susan Blackmore maintains that people who believe they have been abducted by aliens have probably only experienced hallucinations associated with sleep disorders. According to current neurological research, she contends, the feelings of floating commonly reported by alien abductees are produced by electrical activity in the temporal lobes of the brain. People who have such experiences tend to interpret them according to popular cultural myths about extraterrestrials, she argues. Blackmore is a senior lecturer in psychology at the University of the West of England in Bristol.

As you read, consider the following questions:

1. In Blackmore's opinion, why is false memory not the "whole story" behind alien abduction accounts?
2. What two types of sleep disturbance may be related to alien abduction accounts, according to the author?
3. What emotions does Blackmore report feeling during the magnetic field experiment?

From Susan Blackmore, "Alien Abduction: The Inside Story," *New Scientist*, November 19, 1994. All rights reserved. Reprinted by permission of the *New Scientist*.

The outer door slammed shut and a deathly hush descended on the tiny soundproofed room. Half an hour in here, lying in a kind of dentist's reclining chair, might have seemed a restful prospect—except for the converted motorcycle helmet on my head. Embedded in either side of it, just above my ears, were sets of solenoids. Soon these would be delivering pulses of a magnetic field designed to mimic the firing patterns of neurons in the temporal lobes of the brain.

Welcome to the laboratory of Michael Persinger, a neuroscientist at Laurentian University of Sudbury, Ontario. Persinger has long claimed that mystical experiences, out-of-the-body excursions and other psychic experiences are linked in some way to excessive bursts of electrical activity in the temporal lobes. It is known that people vary in what is called "temporal lobe lability". People with high lability have very "unstable" temporal lobes with frequent bursts of electrical activity that can be seen on an EEG (electroencephalograph). Such people tend, he claims, to be anxious and judgemental as well as artistic. People with low lability, by contrast, rarely show bursts of activity in their temporal lobes and are much less imaginative.

Temporal Lobe Lability and Mystical Experiences

Researchers don't need expensive EEG tests to measure temporal lobe lability. Instead they can use questionnaires designed to test a wide range of experiences and beliefs, from déjà vu to headaches. In a series of studies of this kind, questioning about several hundred people in all, Persinger has found that people with high lability more frequently report sensations of floating, flying or leaving the body as well as mystical and psychic experiences. At the extreme end of the scale are people with temporal lobe epilepsy. Their temporal lobes produce the violent, synchronised electrical activity associated with seizures—and sometimes they too report déjà vu, mystical feelings, odd sensations or hallucinations just before a seizure.

One final connection may be that abnormal temporal lobe activity can occur in response to a lack of oxygen. Persinger is one of several scientists who have argued that this is why people who come close to death experience tunnels, lights and sensations of leaving the body.

In the end, however, these observations are nothing more than correlations. They don't prove that neural activity in the temporal lobes causes psychic experiences—or even that it is an effect of psychic experience. What has been missing is a direct demonstration that specific experiences can be created by specific firing of neurons in this part of the brain. Hence the soundproofed room, helmet and magnetic pulses. Persinger believed that by applying magnetic fields across the brain, he could cause bursts of firing in the temporal lobes—bursts just like those associated with the odd experiences. If he could produce the experiences this way, the link with the temporal lobes would be certain.

ALIEN ABDUCTIONS

The reason I was willing to subject myself to this procedure was not just idle curiosity. The BBC's [British Broadcasting Corporation] science programme *Horizon* had asked me to investigate the origin of the latest American craze in crazy experience—abduction by aliens. The details vary. Not everyone claims to have been taken from their bedroom. Some report abductions from their cars or in the street. And many abductees, although not all, say that they saw children or babies while they were "away". Despite that, the stories are more remarkable for their consistency than their differences. A typical report might run as follows.

"I woke up in the middle of the night and everything looked odd and strangely lit. At the end of my bed was a 4 feet high grey alien. Its spindly, thin body supported a huge head with two enormous, slanted, liquid black eyes. It compelled me, telepathically, to follow and led me into a spaceship, along curved corridors to an examination room full of tables on which other people lay. I was forced to lie down while they painfully examined me, extracted ova (or sperm) and implanted something in my nose. I could see jars containing half-human, half-alien fetuses and a nursery full of silent, sickly children. When I eventually found myself back in bed, several hours had gone by."

CHARACTERISTICS OF ALIEN ABDUCTEES

Some abductees recall their experiences in full detail, but for many the "memories" emerge only when they take themselves to a therapist for hypnotic regression. These tales are easy to mock. Why do the aliens always pick Americans? How come they are clever enough to teleport through walls, and to read and erase our memories—but all we have to do to defeat them is a little hypnosis? And if they really put implants in people's noses, how come these always seem to be sneezed out?

Maybe abduction accounts are merely the delusions of the disturbed or the mentally ill. This is easy to counter. Studies of abductees have shown that they are of at least average intelligence, from a wide range of social classes and show no particular signs of mental disturbance or pathology. So what is the explanation? Are alien abduction stories telling us something about the way the mind works?

The fundamental question for neuroscience is the precise relationship between subjective experience and neural firing. In some cases things are relatively simple. A flash of light, for example, produces a cascade of electrical responses at the back of the cortex, while listening to someone speak produces a burst of activity in the left hemisphere. Far less obvious, though, is how patterns of brain activity produce complex subjective states—such as the sensation of having been abducted by an alien.

FALSE MEMORIES OF ALIEN ABDUCTION

Things are complicated by the fact that some abductees only "recall" their experiences under hypnosis. Maybe the hypnotists implanted the ideas, creating "memories" of things that never happened. This takes us to the broader issue of "false memories". The key thing here is that "false memories" are not so different from "true memories". In a sense, all memories are false. There is no tape recorder in the brain. Rather, research suggests that we use stored information to reconstruct accounts of past events. When we retell those events, it is easy to recall our own retelling more clearly than the original experience—even if we've exaggerated it a bit along the way. How, then, can we decide which memories were "real" and which imagined? There is no magic way to the right answer, and some theorists think it just depends on how readily available an image is. If it is clear and detailed and easy to bring to mind, it will be remembered as "real".

When memory is seen this way the phenomenon of false memory seems less bizarre. Take recent experiments by Elizabeth Loftus, a psychologist from Seattle, Washington. She invited volunteers into her laboratory and tried to implant in them the "memory" of being lost in a shopping mall as a young child. The subjects had never actually been lost this way (as far as anyone knew) but their relatives took part by "reminding" them of the event. Afterwards the subjects "remembered" the events clearly and, even when Loftus tried to debrief them, some remained convinced that it had happened.

What does this tell us about alien abductions? First, we must not be diverted by the red herring of hypnosis. Not all abductees are hypnotised, and "false memories" can be created without hypnosis. If you come up with a fantasy of an abduction, then you may well recall it as though it is real whether or not hypnosis is involved.

However, false memory cannot be the whole story. In general, we are quite good at distinguishing fantasy from reality, in spite of the blurred edges, and we do not create false memories entirely out of the blue. Even if false memory plays a role in alien abduction episodes, wouldn't there have to be some kind of core event to build the fantasies around? If so, what might this event be?

THE ROLE OF SLEEP PARALYSIS

One suggestion is sleep paralysis. During normal REM (rapid eye movement) sleep, when the majority of dreams occur, the skeletal muscles are paralysed. This is presumably so that we do not act out our dreams, as animals have been shown to do when the brain centres controlling sleep are suppressed. Normally, we are unaware of this, but occasionally we can become mentally alert while the paralysis persists. Waking up this way can be extremely unpleasant. Yet it is quite common; surveys show that about 20 per cent of people have experienced sleep paralysis at some time or another. Trying to move—and failing—makes it worse and often provokes the sense that there is someone or something trying to squash, strangle or suffocate you. Sexual arousal during dreams is common and may add a particularly powerful edge to the experience.

ABDUCTION STORIES AND POPULAR IMAGERY

Is it possible that people in all times and places occasionally experience vivid, realistic hallucinations, often with sexual content—with the details filled in by the prevailing cultural idioms, sucked out of the *Zeitgeist?* When everyone knows that gods regularly come down to Earth, we hallucinate gods; when everyone knows about demons, it's incubi and succubi; when fairies are widely believed, we see fairies; when the old myths fade and we begin thinking that alien beings are plausible, then that's where our hypnagogic imagery tends. It is striking how similar many of the abduction accounts are now, and how little we hear about incubi and fairies. But it might not be altogether surprising that, in our time and society, short, gray aliens with breeding programs on their minds are what we mainly reach for when we must describe these hallucinations.

Carl Sagan, *Parade* magazine, March 7, 1993.

Some cultures have built elaborate myths around sleep paralysis. Fabled demons, the incubus and succubus, come to have sex with their unwilling victims in the dead of night, and during the Middle Ages many a virgin or nun was reputedly visited by the evil incubi who came to tempt them. In myths common in Newfoundland, the Old Hag comes and presses on sleepers' chests, suffocating them and preventing them from moving. And the hill people of Laos and Vietnam talk of a Grey Ghost who paralyses victims in the dark.

Alien abductions may just be a modern equivalent of a sleep paralysis myth. It makes sense that in late 20th-century Western culture the spaceship and the alien would form its basis. But why the odd lights and other consistent features?

Eerie lighting is common in another kind of sleep disturbance—the false awakening—in which you dream you have woken up. Although you are convinced you are awake, things don't look quite right and familiar objects can seem lit from within. In this state anything is possible because you are still dreaming, but the apparent familiarity of the environment means that the experiences are more likely to be interpreted as real. This is one variety of what Celia Green, a parapsychologist with an independent laboratory in Oxford, refers to as a "metachoric experience", where the perceived world is replaced by an imagined replica.

A link between sleep disturbance and apparent abductions is lent some support by the research of the late Nicholas Spanos and his colleagues at Carleton University in Ottawa. They compared groups of people who had had intense UFO experiences, such as abduction, with those who had had less intense experiences and found that the former were more often related to sleep.

FEELINGS OF FLOATING OR FLYING EXPLAINED

But even if sleep phenomena are part of the answer, that doesn't explain the sense of being taken away bodily, of flying or floating and going on a journey. Enter Persinger and his idea that abduction-like experiences are caused by complex patterns of activity in the temporal lobes. He argues that people with very labile temporal lobes will naturally have such experiences from time to time. These are particularly likely to occur during sleep and so these people might easily wake up with odd bodily sensations and feelings of floating or flying.

In addition, magnetic effects from earthquakes could be strong enough to set off the necessary firing. To test this he looked for, and found, a strong link between the dates of seismic events and claims of UFO sightings, abductions and other strange phenomena from past centuries. Nor can hysteria and fear be the sole explanations, he argues. Reports of strange experiences peaked in the weeks and months before earthquakes, says Persinger, when magnetic changes might have been happening, but little else to suggest an imminent seismic event.

Those who believe that abductions really happen have tried to counter this theory by showing that abductees do not score higher on measures of temporal lobe lability. But arguments have raged over whether enough people were tested, and whether their experiences were really abductions. Now, in a bid to settle the issue, Persinger is turning to direct simulations. And this is where my experiences in the lab chamber come into the picture.

An Experience Created in a Laboratory

I was wide awake throughout. Nothing seemed to happen for the first ten minutes or so. Instructed to describe aloud anything that happened, I felt under pressure to say something, anything. Then suddenly my doubts vanished. "I'm swaying. It's like being on a hammock." Then it felt for all the world as though two hands had grabbed my shoulders and were bodily yanking me upright. I knew I was still lying in the reclining chair, but someone, or something, was pulling me up.

Something seemed to get hold of my leg and pull it, distort it, and drag it up the wall. It felt as though I had been stretched half way up to the ceiling. Then came the emotions. Totally out of the blue, but intensely and vividly, I suddenly felt angry—not just mildly cross but that clear-minded anger out of which you act—but there was nothing and no one to act on. After perhaps ten seconds, it was gone. Later, it was replaced by an equally sudden attack of fear. I was terrified—of nothing in particular. The long-term medical effects of applying strong magnetic fields to the brain are largely unknown, but I felt weak and disoriented for a couple of hours after coming out of the chamber.

Of course, I knew that it was all caused by the magnetic field changes, but what would people feel if such things happened spontaneously in the middle of the night? Wouldn't they want, above all, to find an explanation, to find out who had been doing it to them? If someone told them an alien was responsible and invited them to join an abductees' support group, wouldn't some of them seize on the idea, if only to reassure themselves that they weren't going mad? One last thought. Persinger applied a silent and invisible force to my brain and created a specific experience for me. He claimed that he was imitating the basic sequences of the processes of memory and perception and that, by varying those sequences, he could control my experience. Could he have done it from a distance? Could it be done on a wider scale? Suddenly prospects of magnetic mind control seem an awful lot worse than the idea of being abducted by imaginary aliens.

| "There's no doubt that the U.S. government has been less than forthcoming on the topic of UFOs."

THE U.S. GOVERNMENT IS COVERING UP EVIDENCE OF UFOS

Dennis Stacy

In 1947, debris from a crashed object was recovered near Roswell, New Mexico; many UFO researchers believe it was the remains of an extraterrestrial spacecraft, though the air force maintains that it was a weather balloon. Dennis Stacy contends in the following viewpoint that the Roswell incident provides the best evidence that the U.S. government has been covering up its knowledge and study of the existence of extraterrestrial visitors. The military's reluctance to release documents about UFOs sought by researchers using the Freedom of Information Act, he argues, suggests that the government is hiding something. Stacy is editor of the *MUFON UFO Journal*, published by the Mutual UFO Network.

As you read, consider the following questions:

1. According to Stacy, what does the Roswell incident symbolize, whether it is real or not?
2. Why is government secrecy dangerous in Steven Aftergood's opinion, as quoted by the author?
3. According to the author, what hidden agenda might the air force have for maintaining the "Cosmic Watergate"?

From Dennis Stacy, "Cosmic Conspiracy: Six Decades of Government UFO Cover-ups, Part 1," Omni, April 1994. Reprinted by permission of Omni, ©1994, Omni Publications International, Ltd.

Lightning flashed over Corona, New Mexico, and thunder rattled the thin windowpanes of the small shack where ranch foreman Mac Brazel slept. Brazel was used to summer thunderstorms, but he was suddenly brought wide awake by a loud explosion that set the dishes in the kitchen sink dancing. *Sonofabitch,* he thought to himself before sinking back to sleep, *the sheep will be scattered halfway between hell and high water come dawn.*

In the morning, Brazel rode out on horseback, accompanied by seven-year-old Timothy Proctor, to survey the damage. According to published accounts, Brazel and young Proctor stumbled across something unearthly—a field of tattered debris two to three hundred yards wide stretching some three-quarters of a mile in length. No rocket scientist, Brazel still realized he had something strange on his hands—so strange that he decided to haul several pieces of it into Roswell, some 75 miles distant, a day or two later.

A Crashed UFO?

For all its lightness, the debris in Brazel's pickup bed seemed remarkably durable. Sheriff George Wilcox reportedly took one look at it and called the military at Roswell Army Air Field, then home to the world's only atomic-bomb wing. Two officers from the base eventually arrived and agreed to accompany Brazel back to the debris field.

As a consequence of their investigation, a press release unique in the history of the American military appeared on the front page of the *Roswell Daily Record* for July 8, 1947. Authored by public-information officer Lt. Walter Haut and approved by base commander Col. William Blanchard, it admitted that the many rumors regarding UFOs "became a reality yesterday when the intelligence officer of the 509th Bomb Group of the Eighth Air Force, Roswell Army Air Field, was fortunate enough to gain possession of a disc through the cooperation of one of the local ranchers and the sheriff's office of Chaves County."

Haut's noon press release circled the planet, reprinted in papers as far abroad as Germany and England, where it was picked up by the prestigious *London Times*. UFOs were real! Media calls poured in to the *Roswell Daily Record* and the local radio station, which had first broken the news, demanding additional details.

Four hours later and some 600 miles to the east in Fort Worth, Texas, Brig. Gen. Roger Ramey, commander of the Eighth Air Force, held press conference to answer reporters' questions. Spread on the general's office floor were lumps of a blackened, rubberlike material and crumpled pieces of what looked like a flimsy tinfoil kite. Ramey posed for pictures, kneeling on his carpet with the material, as did Maj. Jesse Marcel, flown in from Roswell for the occasion. Alas, allowed the general, the Roswell incident was a simple case of mistaken identity; in reality, the so-called recovered flying disc was nothing more than a weather balloon with an attached radar reflector.

THE GOVERNMENT'S COVER-UP OF UFOS

"Unfortunately, the media bought the Air Force cover-up hook, line, and sinker," asserts Stanton Friedman, a nuclear physicist and coauthor with aviation writer Don Berliner of *Crash at Corona*, one of three books written about Roswell. "The weather-balloon story went in the next morning's paper, the phone calls dropped off dramatically, and any chance of an immediate follow-up was effectively squelched."

Ramey's impromptu press conference marks the beginning of what Friedman refers to as a "'Cosmic Watergate,' the ongoing cover-up of the government's knowledge about extraterrestrial UFOs and their terrestrial activities." By contrast, says Friedman, the original Watergate snafu and cover-up pales in significance. In fact, if Friedman and his cohorts within the UFO community are correct, military involvement in the recovery of a crashed flying saucer would rank as the most well-kept and explosive secret in world history.

Of course, not all students of the subject see it that way. "You have to put Roswell in a certain context," cautions Curtis Peebles, an aerospace historian whose treatment of UFOs as an evolving belief system in *Watch the Skies!* was published in 1994 by the Smithsonian Institution. "And the relevant context is the role of government and its relationship to the governed. Americans have always been suspicious, if not actively contemptuous, of their government. On the other hand, forget what the government says and look at what it does. Is there any evidence in the historical record that the Air Force or government behaved as if it actually owned a flying saucer presumably thousands of years in advance of anything on either the Soviet or U.S. side? If there is, I didn't find it."

Regardless of its ultimate reality, however, Roswell symbolizes the difficulties and frustrations Friedman and fellow UFOlogists have encountered in prying loose what the government does or does not know about UFOs. Memories fade, documents get lost or misplaced, witnesses die, and others refuse to speak up, either out of fear of ridicule or, according to Friedman, because of secrecy oaths. Despite a trail that lay cold for more than 30 years,

UFOlogists still consider Roswell one of the most convincing UFO cases on record. In 1978, for example, Friedman personally interviewed Maj. Jesse Marcel shortly before his death. "He still didn't know what the material was," says Friedman, "except that it was like nothing he had ever seen before and certainly wasn't from any weather balloon." According to what Marcel reportedly told Friedman, in fact, the featherlight material couldn't be dented by a sledgehammer or burned by a blowtorch.

THE AIR FORCE'S OFFICIAL INVESTIGATION OF UFOs

Yet getting the Air Force itself to say anything about Roswell in particular or UFOs in general can be an exercise in futility. Officials are either bureaucratically vague or maddeningly abrupt. Maj. David Thurston, a Pentagon spokesperson for the Air Force Office of Public Affairs, could only refer inquiries to the Air Force Historical Research Center in Montgomery, Alabama, where unit histories are kept on microfilm for public review. But a spokesperson there said they had no "investigative material" and suggested checking the National Archives for files from Project Blue Book, the Air Force's public UFO investigative agency from the late 1940s until its closure in December of 1969.

Indeed, the dismissive nature with which U.S. officials treated Blue Book research seemed to indicate they were unimpressed; on that point, believers and skeptics alike agree. But according to Friedman and colleagues, that demeanor, and Blue Book itself, was a ruse. Instead, far from the eyes of Blue Book patsies, in top-secret meetings of upper-echelon intelligence officers from military and civilian agencies alike, UFOs—including real crashed saucers and the mangled bodies of aliens—were the subject of endless study and debate. What's more, claims Friedman, proof of this UFO reality can be found in the classified files of government vaults.

With all this documentation, Friedman might have had a field day. Unfortunately, researchers had no mechanism for forcing classified documents to the surface until 1966, when Congress passed the Freedom of Information Act (FOIA). The FOIA was later amended in the last year of the Nixon administration (1974) to include the Privacy Act. Now individuals could view their own files, and some UFOlogists—Friedman included—were surprised to find that their personal UFO activities had resulted in government dossiers.

But that as it may, UFOlogists saw the FOIA as a means to end, and beginning in the 1970s, their requests and lawsuits started pouring in. Attorneys for the Connecticut-based Citizens

Against UFO Secrecy (CAUS) and other UFO activities eventually unleashed a flood tide of previously classified UFO documents.

In many cases, notes Barry Greenwood, director of research for CAUS and coauthor with Lawrence Fawcett of *The Government UFO Cover-up*, most agencies at first denied they had any such documents in their files. "A case in point is the CIA," says Greenwood, "which assured us that its interest and involvement in UFOs ended in 1953. After a lengthy lawsuit, the CIA ultimately released more than a thousand pages of documents. To date, we've acquired more than ten thousand documents pertaining to UFOs, the overwhelming majority of which were from the CIA, FBI, Air Force, and various other military agencies. It's safe to say there are probably that many more we haven't seen."

UFO DOCUMENTS RELEASED BY THE GOVERNMENT

As might be expected, the UFO paper trail is a mixed bag. Many of the documents released are simple sighting reports logged well after the demise of Blue Book. Others are more tantalizing. A document released by the North American Aerospace Defense Command (NORAD) revealed that several sensitive military bases scattered from Maine to Montana were temporarily put on alert status following a series of sightings in October and November of 1975. An Air Force Office of Special Intelligence document reported a landed light seen near Kirtland Air Force Base, Albuquerque, New Mexico, on the night of August 8, 1980.

Another warm and still-smoking gun, according to Greenwood, is the so-called Bolender memo, named after its author, Brig. Gen. C.H. Bolender, then Air Force deputy director of development. Dated October 20, 1969, it expressly states that "reports of unidentified flying objects which could affect national security . . . are not part of the Blue Book system." Says Greenwood, "I take that to mean that Blue Book was little more than an exercise in public relations. The really significant reports went somewhere else. Where did they go? That's what we would like to know."

Of course there are objections to such a literal interpretation. "As I understand the context in which it was written," says Philip Klass, a former senior editor with *Aviation Week and Space Technology* and author of *UFOs: The Public Deceived*, "the Bolender memo tried to address the problem of what would happen with UFO reports of any sort following the closure of Project Blue Book. Bolender was simply saying that other channels for such reports, be they incoming Soviet missiles or whatever, already existed."

Greenwood counters that the original memo speaks for itself, adding that "the interesting thing is that sixteen referenced attachments are presently reported as missing from Air Force files."

Naturally, there was a bit of skepticism among the media regarding the official Air Force explanation.

Rubes is reprinted by permission of Leigh Rubin and Creators Syndicate.

Missing file are one problem. Files known to exist but kept under wraps, notes Greenwood, are another. To make his point, he cites a case involving the ultrasecret National Security Agency, or NSA, an acronym often assumed by insiders to mean "Never Say Anything." Using cross references found in CIA and other intelligence-agency papers, CAUS attorneys filed for the release of all NSA documents pertaining to the UFO phenomenon. After initial denials, the NSA admitted to the existence of some 160 such documents but resisted their release on the grounds of national security.

Federal District Judge Gerhard Gesell upheld the NSA's request for suppression following a review (judge's chambers only) of the agency's classified 21-page In Camera petition. "Two years later," Greenwood says, "we finally got a copy of the NSA In Camera affidavit. Of 582 lines, 412 or approximately 75 percent, were completely blacked out. The government can't have it both ways. Either UFOs affect national security or they don't."

The NSA's blockage of the CAUS suit only highlights the shortcomings of the Freedom of Information Act, according to Friedman. "The American public operates under the illusion that the FOIA is some sort of magical key that will unlock all of the government's secret vaults," he says, "that all you have to do is ask. They also seem to think everything is in one one big computer file somewhere deep in the bowels of the Pentagon, when nothing could be farther from the truth. Secrecy thrives on compartmentalization."

FIGHTING GOVERNMENT SECRECY

In recent years, UFOlogist have found an unusual ally in the person of Steven Aftergood, an electrical engineer who directs the Project on Government and Secrecy for the Washington, DC–based Federation of American Scientists, where most members wouldn't ordinarily give UFOs the time of day. "Our problem," says Aftergood, "is with government secrecy on principle, because it widens the gap between citizens and government, making it that much more difficult to participate in the democratic process. It's also antithetical to peer review and cross-fertilization, two natural processes conducive to the growth of both science and technology. Bureaucratic secrecy is also prohibitively expensive."

Aftergood cites some daunting statistics in his favor. Despite campaign promises by a succession of Democratic and Republican presidential administrations to make government files more publicly accessible, more than 300 million documents compiled prior to 1960 in the National Archives alone still await declassification. Aftergood also points to a 1990 Department of Defense study, which estimated the cost of protecting industrial—not military—secrets at almost $14 billion a year. "That's a budget about the size of NASA's," he says, adding that "the numbers were ludicrous enough during the Cold War, but now that the

Cold War is supposedly over, they're even more ludicrous."

Could the Air Force and other government agencies have their own hidden agenda for maintaining the reputed Cosmic Watergate? Yes, according to some pundits who say UFOs may be our own advanced super-top-secret aerial platforms, not extraterrestrial vehicles from on high. Something of the sort could be occurring at the supersecret Groom Lake test facility in Nevada, part of the immense Nellis Air Force Base gunnery range north of Las Vegas. Aviation buffs believe the Groom Lake runway, one of the world's longest, could be home to the much-rumored *Aurora*, reputed to be a hypersonic Mach-8 spy plane and a replacement for the retired SR-71 Blackbird.

In fact, the Air Force routinely denies the existence of *Aurora*. And with Blue Book a closed chapter, it no longer has to hold press conferences to answer reporters' questions about UFOs. From the government's perspective, the current confusion between terrestrial technology and extraterrestrial UFOs could be a marriage of both coincidence and convenience. The Air Force doesn't seem to be taking chances. On September 30, 1993, it initiated procedures to seize another 3,900 acres adjoining Groom Lake, effectively sealing off two public viewing sites of a base it refuses to admit exists.

UFO REPORTS MASK MILITARY OPERATIONS

By perpetuating such disinformation, if that is, in fact, what's happening, the Air Force might be using a page torn from the Soviet Union's Cold War playbook. James Oberg, a senior space engineer and author of *Red Star in Orbit*, a critical analysis of the Soviet space program, has long argued that Soviet officials remained publicly mum about widely reported Russian UFOs in the 1970s and 1980s because such reports masked military operations conducted at the supersecret Plesetsk Cosmodrome. "Could a similar scenario occur in this country? It's conceivable," concedes Oberg. "On the other hand, should our own government take an interest in UFO reports, especially those that may reflect missile or space technology from around the world? Sure. I'd be dismayed if we didn't. But does it follow that alien-acquired technology recovered at Roswell is driving our own space technology program? I don't see any outstanding evidence for it."

Friedman's counterargument is not so much a technological as a political one. "Governments and nations demand allegiance in order to survive," he says. "They don't want us thinking in global terms, as a citizen of a planet as opposed to a particular political entity, because that would threaten their very existence. The impact on our collective social, economic, and religious structures of admitting that we have been contacted by another intelligent life form would be enormous if not literally catastrophic to the political powers that be."

Whatever its reason for holding large numbers of documents and an array of information close to the vest, there's no doubt that the U.S. government has been less than forthcoming on the topic of UFOs. Historically, the government's public attitude toward UFOs has run the gamut of human emotions, at times confused and dismissive, at others deliberately covert and coy. On one hand, it claims to have recovered a flying disc; on the other, a weather balloon. One night UFOs constitute a threat to the national security; the next they are merely part of a public hysteria based on religious feelings, fear of technology, mass hypnosis, or whatever the prevailing psychology of the era will bear.

"Research located no records at existing Air Force offices that indicated any 'cover-up' by the USAF or any indication of [the] recovery [of an extraterrestrial spacecraft]."

THE U.S. GOVERNMENT IS NOT COVERING UP EVIDENCE OF UFOS

Richard L. Weaver and James McAndrew

In 1994, Congressman Steven Schiff officially requested a review of military records and the release of any documents pertaining to the crash of a UFO near Roswell, New Mexico, in 1947. Richard L. Weaver and James McAndrew, the air force officers who conducted the review, report in the following viewpoint that the military does not possess any records indicating that the Roswell incident was the crash of an extraterrestrial spacecraft. The most likely explanation for the incident was the crash of a research balloon, they contend. Further, Weaver and McAndrew argue, there is no evidence to suggest that the government has covered up the existence of extraterrestrial spacecraft, as UFO enthusiasts maintain. Weaver, a colonel, is the director of security and special program oversight for the secretary of the air force. McAndrew, a first lieutenant, is a declassification and review officer.

As you read, consider the following questions:

1. When did the modern preoccupation with UFOs begin, according to Weaver and McAndrew?
2. Why was the air force seriously concerned with UFOs during the 1940s and 1950s, according to the authors?
3. In the authors' opinion, how would the military have reacted if an extraterrestrial spacecraft had crashed at Roswell in 1947?

From "The Roswell Report: Fact Versus Fiction in the New Mexico Desert," (written by Richard L. Weaver and James McAndrew on behalf of) Headquarters United States Air Force (Washington, DC: Government Printing Office, 1995).

The "Roswell Incident" refers to an event that supposedly happened in July, 1947, wherein the Army Air Forces (AAF) allegedly recovered remains of a crashed "flying disc" near Roswell, New Mexico. In February, 1994, the General Accounting Office (GAO), acting on the request of New Mexico Congressman Steven Schiff, initiated an audit to attempt to locate records of such an incident and to determine if records regarding it were properly handled. Although the GAO effort was to look at a number of government agencies, the apparent focus was on the United States Air Force (USAF). The Director, Security and Special Program Oversight, Office of the Secretary of the Air Force (SAF/AAZ), as the Central Point of Contact for the GAO in this matter, initiated a systematic search of current Air Force offices as well as numerous archives and records centers that might help explain this matter. Research revealed that the "Roswell Incident" was not even considered a UFO event until the 1978–1980 time frame. Prior to that, the incident was dismissed because the AAF originally identified the debris recovered as being that of a weather balloon. Subsequently, various authors wrote a number of books claiming that not only was debris from an alien spacecraft recovered, but also the bodies of the craft's alien occupants. These claims continue to evolve today and the Air Force is now routinely accused of engaging in a "cover-up" of this supposed event.

An Official Explanation of the Roswell Crash

The research located no records at existing Air Force offices that indicated any "cover-up" by the USAF or any indication of such a recovery. Consequently, efforts were intensified by Air Force researchers at numerous locations where records for the period in question were stored. The records reviewed did not reveal any increase in operations, security, or any other activity in July, 1947, that indicated any such unusual event may have occurred. Records were located and thoroughly explored concerning a then–Top Secret balloon project, designed to attempt to monitor Soviet nuclear tests, known as Project Mogul. Additionally, several surviving project personnel were located and interviewed, as was the only surviving person who recovered debris from the original Roswell site in 1947 and the former officer who initially identified the wreckage as a balloon. Comparison of all information developed or obtained indicated that the material recovered near Roswell was consistent with a balloon device and most likely from one of the Mogul balloons that had not been previously recovered. Air Force research efforts did not disclose any records of the recovery of any "alien" bodies or extraterrestrial materials. . . .

WHAT WAS ORIGINALLY REPORTED IN 1947

The modern preoccupation with what ultimately came to be called Unidentified Flying Objects (UFOs) actually began in June, 1947. Although some pro-UFO researchers argue that sightings of UFOs go back to Biblical times, most researchers will not dispute that anything in UFO history can compare with the phenomenon that began in 1947. What was later characterized as "the UFO Wave of 1947" began with 16 alleged sightings that occurred between May 17 and July 12, 1947 (although some researchers claim there were as many as 800 sightings during that period). Interestingly, the "Roswell Incident" was not considered one of these 1947 events until the 1978–1980 time frame. There is no dispute, however, that something happened near Roswell in July, 1947, since it was reported in a number of contemporary newspaper articles, the most famous of which were the July 8 and July 9 editions of the *Roswell Daily Record*. The July 8 edition reported "RAAF Captures Flying Saucer On Ranch In Roswell Region," while the next day's edition reported, "Ramey Empties Roswell Saucer" and "Harassed Rancher Who Located 'Saucer' Sorry He Told About It."

The first story reported that the Intelligence Officer of the 509th Bomb Group, stationed at Roswell Army Air Field, Major Jesse A. Marcel, had recovered a "flying disc" from the range lands of an unidentified rancher in the vicinity of Roswell and that the disc had been "flown to higher headquarters." That same story also reported that a Roswell couple claimed to have seen a large unidentified object fly by their home on July 2, 1947.

THE "FLYING DISC"

The July 9 edition of the paper noted that Brigadier General Roger Ramey, Commander of the Eighth Air Force at Forth Worth, Texas, stated that upon examination the debris recovered by Marcel was determined to be a weather balloon. The wreckage was described as a ". . . bundle of tinfoil, broken wood beams, and rubber remnants of a balloon. . . ." The additional story of the "harassed rancher" identified him as W.W. Brazel of Lincoln County, New Mexico. He claimed that he and his son, Vernon, found the material on June 14, 1947, when they "came upon a large area of bright wreckage made up of rubber strips, tinfoil, a rather tough paper, and sticks." He picked up some of the debris on July 4 and ". . . the next day he first heard about the flying discs and wondered if what he had found might have been the remnants of one of these." Brazel subsequently went to Roswell on July 7 and contacted the Sheriff, who apparently notified Major Marcel. Major Marcel and "a man in plain clothes" then accompanied Brazel home to pick up the rest of the pieces. The article further related that Brazel thought that the material:

> . . . might have been as large as a table top. The balloon which held it up, if that is how it worked, must have been about 12 feet long, he felt, measuring the distance by the size of the room in which he sat. The rubber was smoky gray in color and scattered over an area about 200 yards in diameter. When the debris was gathered up the tinfoil, paper, tape, and sticks made a bundle about three feet long and 7 or 8 inches thick, while the rubber made a bundle about 18 or 20 inches long and about 8 inches thick. In all, he estimated, the entire lot would have weighed maybe five pounds. There was no sign of any metal in the area which might have been used for an engine and no sign of any propellers of any kind. Although at least one paper fin had been glued onto some of the tinfoil. There were no words to be found anywhere on the instrument although there were letters on some of the parts. Considerable scotch tape and some tape with flowers printed upon it had been used in the construction. No string or wire were to be found but there were some eyelets in the paper to indicate that some sort of attachment may have been used. Brazel said that he had previously found two weather balloons on the ranch, but that what he found this time did not in any way resemble either of these.

EVOLUTION OF THE EVENT FROM 1947 TO THE PRESENT

General Ramey's press conference and rancher Brazel's statement effectively ended this as a UFO-related matter until 1978, although some UFO researchers argue that there were several obtuse references to it in 1950s-era literature. Roswell, for example, is not referred to in the official USAF investigation of UFOs reported in Project Bluebook or its predecessors, Project Sign and Project Grudge, which ran from 1948–1969 (which Congressman Schiff subsequently learned when he made his original inquiry).

In 1978, an article appeared in a tabloid newspaper, the *National Enquirer*, which reported the former intelligence officer, Marcel, claimed that he had recovered UFO debris near Roswell in 1947. Also in 1978, a UFO researcher, Stanton Friedman, met with Marcel and began investigating the claims that the material Marcel handled was from a crashed UFO. Similarly, two authors, William L. Moore and Charles Berlitz, also engaged in research which led them to publish a book, *The Roswell Incident*, in 1980. In this book they reported they interviewed a number of persons who claimed to have been present at Roswell in 1947 and professed to be either firsthand or secondhand witnesses to strange events that supposedly occurred. Since 1978–1980, other UFO researchers, most notably Donald Schmitt and Kevin Randle [authors of *The UFO Crash at Roswell*], claim to have located and interviewed even more persons with supposed knowledge of unusual happenings at Roswell. These included both civilian and former military persons.

Additionally, the Robert Stack–hosted television show "Unsolved Mysteries" devoted a large portion of one show to a "recreation" of the supposed Roswell events. Numerous other television shows have done likewise, and a made-for-TV movie on the subject is due to be released this summer [1995]. The overall thrust of these articles, books, and shows is that the "Roswell Incident" was actually the crash of a craft from another world, the US Government recovered it, and has been "covering up" this fact from the American public since 1947, using a combination of disinformation, ridicule, and threats of bodily harm, to do so. Generally, the USAF bears the brunt of these accusations. . . .

WHAT THE ROSWELL INCIDENT WAS NOT

The Air Force research found absolutely no indication that what happened near Roswell in 1947 involved any type of extraterrestrial spacecraft. This, of course, is the crux of this entire matter. "Pro-UFO" persons who obtain a copy of this report, at this point, most probably begin the "cover-up is still on" claims. Nevertheless, the research indicated absolutely no evidence of *any* kind that a spaceship crashed near Roswell or that any alien occupants were recovered therefrom, in some secret military operation or otherwise. This does not mean, however, that the early Air Force was not concerned about UFOs. However, in the early days, "UFO" meant Unidentified Flying Object, which literally translated as some object in the air that was not readily identifiable. It did not mean, as the term has evolved in today's language, to equate to alien spaceships. Records from the period reviewed by Air Force researchers, as well as those cited by the authors mentioned before, do indicate that the USAF *was* seriously concerned about the inability to adequately identify unknown flying objects reported in American airspace. All the records, however, indicated that the focus of concern was not on aliens, hostile or otherwise, but on the Soviet Union. Many documents from that period speak to the possibility of developmental secret Soviet aircraft overflying US airspace. This, of course, was of major concern to the fledgling USAF, whose job it was to protect these same skies.

The research revealed only one official AAF document that indicated that there was any activity of any type that pertained to UFOs and Roswell in July, 1947. This was a small section of the July Historical Report for the 509th Bomb Group and Roswell Army Air Field that stated: "The Office of Public Information was quite busy during the month answering inquiries on the 'flying disc,' which was reported to be in possession of the 509th Bomb Group. The object turned out to be a radar tracking balloon." Additionally, this history showed that the 509th Commander, Colonel Blanchard, went on leave on July 8, 1947, which would be a somewhat unusual maneuver for a person involved in the supposed first ever recovery of extraterrestrial materials. (Detractors claim Blanchard did this as a ploy to elude the press and go to the scene to direct the recovery operations.) The history and the morning reports also showed that the subsequent activities at Roswell during the month were mostly mundane and not indicative of any unusual high-level activity, expenditure of manpower, resources or security.

NO INDICATION OF UNUSUAL ACTIVITY

Likewise, the researchers found no indication of heightened activity anywhere else in the military hierarchy in the July, 1947, message traffic or orders (to include classified traffic). There were no indications and warnings, notice of alerts, or a higher tempo of operational activity reported that would be logically generated if an alien craft, whose intentions were unknown, entered US territory. To believe that such operational and high-level security activity could be conducted solely by relying on unsecured telecommunications or personal contact without creating any records of such activity certainly stretches the imagination of those who have served in the military who know that paperwork of some kind is necessary to accomplish even emergency, highly classified, or sensitive tasks.

An example of activity sometimes cited by pro-UFO writers to illustrate the point that something unusual was going on was the travel of Lieutenant General Nathan Twining, Commander of the Air Materiel Command, to New Mexico in July, 1947. Actually, records were located indicating that Twining went to the Bomb Commanders' Course on July 8, along with a number of other general officers, and requested orders to do so a month before, on June 5, 1947.

Similarly, it has also been alleged that General Hoyt Vandenberg, Deputy Chief of Staff at the time, had been involved in directing activity regarding events at Roswell. Activity reports, located in General Vandenberg's personal papers stored in the Library of Congress, did indicate that on July 7, he was busy with a "flying disc" incident; however this particular incident involved Ellington Field, Texas, and the Spokane (Washington) Depot. After much discussion and information gathering on this incident, it was learned to be a hoax. There is no similar mention of his personal interest or involvement in Roswell events except in the newspapers.

PROJECT MOGUL AND THE ROSWELL INCIDENT

A mysterious 1947 crash in the New Mexico desert that became legendary among flying-saucer fans and cover-up theorists turns out to have involved something nearly as strange as an alien spaceship.

The wreckage, quickly whisked away by the Air Force, was part of an airborne system for atomic-age spying that was invented by a leading geophysicist and developed by Columbia University, New York University and the Woods Hole Oceanographic Institution, according to an Air Force report on the once-secret project as well as principals in the espionage effort.

The program was called Project Mogul, and its goal, set by a postwar America wary of losing its atomic monopoly, was to search high in the atmosphere for weak reverberations from nuclear-test blasts half a world away.

William J. Broad, New York Times, September 18, 1994.

The above are but two small examples that indicate that if some event happened that was one of the "watershed happenings" in human history, the US military certainly reacted in an unconcerned and cavalier manner. In an actual case, the military would have had to order thousands of soldiers and airmen, not only at Roswell but throughout the US, to act nonchalantly, pretend to conduct and report business as usual, and generate absolutely no paperwork of a suspicious nature, while simultaneously anticipating that twenty years or more into the future people would have available a comprehensive Freedom of Information Act that would give them great leeway to review and explore government documents. The records indicate that none of this happened (or if it did, it was controlled by a security system so efficient and tight that no one, US or otherwise, has been able to duplicate it since. If such a system had been in effect at the time, it would have also been used to protect our atomic secrets from the Soviets, which history has showed obviously was not the case.). The records reviewed confirmed that no such sophisticated and efficient security system existed. . . .

THE TOP SECRET BALLOON

The Air Force research did not locate or develop any information that the "Roswell Incident" was a UFO event. All available official materials, although they do not directly address Roswell *per se*, indicate that the most likely source of the wreckage recovered from the Brazel Ranch was from one of the Project MOGUL balloons. Although that project was Top Secret at the time, there was also no specific indication found to indicate an official pre-planned cover story was in place to explain an event such as that which ultimately happened. It appears that the identification of the wreckage as being part of a weather balloon device, as reported in the newspapers at the time, was based on the fact that there was no physical difference in the radar targets and the neoprene balloons (other than the numbers and configuration) between MOGUL balloons and normal weather balloons. Additionally, it seems that there was overreaction by Colonel Blanchard and Major Marcel in originally reporting that a "flying disc" had been recovered. . . .

Likewise, there was no indication in official records from the period that there was heightened military operational or security activity which should have been generated if this was, in fact, the first recovery of materials and/or persons from another world. The postwar US military (or today's for that matter) did not have the capability to rapidly identify, recover, coordinate, cover up, and quickly minimize public scrutiny of such an event. The claim that they did so without leaving even a little bit of a suspicious paper trail for 47 years is incredible.

PERIODICAL BIBLIOGRAPHY

The following articles have been selected to supplement the diverse views presented in this chapter. Addresses are provided for periodicals not indexed in the *Readers' Guide to Periodical Literature*, the *Alternative Press Index*, the *Social Sciences Index*, or the *Index to Legal Periodicals and Books*.

J. Roger P. Angel and Neville J. Woolf "Searching for Life on Other Planets," *Scientific American*, April 1996.

Anne Bernays "Spaced Out—and Other Delusions," *Nation*, June 27, 1994.

Susan Blackmore "Alien Abduction: The Inside Story," *New Scientist*, November 19, 1994.

William J. Broad "Wreckage of a 'Spaceship': Of This Earth (and U.S.)," *New York Times*, September 18, 1994.

Gail S. Cleere "Bagging the Little Green Man," *Natural History*, February 1994.

Missy Daniel "PW Interviews: John E. Mack," *Publishers Weekly*, April 18, 1994.

Kendrick Frazier "UFOs Real? Government Covering Up? Survey Says 50 Percent Think So," *Skeptical Inquirer*, November/December 1995.

J. Antonio Huneeus "UFO Chronicle," *Fate*, July 1996. Available from 84 S. Wabasha, St. Paul, MN 55107.

Michael D. Lemonick "Is Someone Out There?" *Time*, January 29, 1996.

Omni "The Roswell Declaration," October 1994.

Carl Sagan "The Search for Extraterrestrial Life," *Scientific American*, October 1994.

Seth Shostak "Tuning In on Extraterrestrials," *World & I*, June 1995. Available from 3600 New York Ave. NE, Washington, DC 20002.

Dave Thomas "The Roswell Incident and Project Mogul," *Skeptical Inquirer*, July/August 1995.

James Willwerth "The Man from Outer Space," *Time*, April 25, 1994.

CHAPTER 3

Does ESP Exist?

CHAPTER PREFACE

Since the inception of the study of extrasensory perception (ESP) in the 1920s, parapsychologists have been challenged by skeptics to develop a scientific experiment that consistently demonstrates the existence of a psychic phenomenon. In the mid-1980s, parapsychologist Charles Honorton and skeptical psychologist Ray Hyman defined the parameters of such an experiment. In the ganzfeld experiment, a person whose psychic ability is being tested is isolated in a room and subjected to a mild form of sensory deprivation. In a separate room, a sender concentrates on a randomly selected video clip or magazine picture. After half an hour, the receiver is shown four pictures or video clips and is asked to choose the one that most closely fits the mental images he or she perceived while isolated. According to experimenters, the receiver would have a 25-percent chance of guessing the correct picture or video clip. If over a sufficient number of experiments a receiver picks the correct target more than 30 percent of the time, then ESP has been demonstrated, parapsychologists believe.

Jessica Utts, a professor of statistics at the University of California, Davis, argues that ganzfeld experiments present unquestionable evidence that ESP exists. Combining the results of several carefully conducted experiments, she maintains that the number of correctly chosen targets is consistently above 30 percent. Such significant results effectively eliminate chance guessing as an explanation for the phenomenon, Utts contends. The ganzfeld experiments have been successfully replicated enough times, she asserts, to end the dispute over whether ESP has been scientifically proven to exist.

But skeptics do dispute the results of the experiments. In a 1996 article, Sharon Begley, a senior writer for *Newsweek* magazine, reports that skeptics contend that in some experiments parapsychology researchers subtly or unconsciously prompt receivers to choose the correct target, making the results of the experiments invalid. Begley notes that when ganzfeld experiments have been conducted by skeptical researchers, they have failed to produce results that are above the rate of chance guessing. Given such experimental results, skeptics argue, ESP cannot be accepted as a proven phenomenon.

While some scientists assert that ESP has definitely been proven to exist, others object that there is still no incontrovertible evidence to support such a claim. The viewpoints in the following chapter debate whether the existence of ESP and other psychic phenomena has been proven.

| "Many parapsychologists have reported positive psi results using a wide variety of experimental procedures."

THE EXISTENCE OF ESP HAS BEEN PROVEN

Daryl J. Bem

One of the main challenges for parapsychology researchers attempting to prove the existence of ESP and other psychic phenomena (psi) has been to develop an experiment that can be repeated and verified by other scientists. In the following viewpoint, Daryl J. Bem argues that the autoganzfeld procedure, developed jointly by a prominent parapsychologist and a leading skeptic, is a scientific experiment that can be repeated by any researcher. In surveying the results of eleven autoganzfeld experiments, the author finds evidence that ESP has been scientifically proven. Bem is a professor of psychology at Cornell University in Ithaca, New York.

As you read, consider the following questions:

1. How does Bem define psi? What abilities constitute ESP, according to the author?
2. What has been the most serious criticism of parapsychology, in the author's view?
3. According to the author, what does the word *ganzfeld* mean? How is a ganzfeld experiment set up?

From Daryl J. Bem, "Does ESP Exist?" This article first appeared in the August 1994 issue and is reprinted by permission of the *World* & I, a publication of The Washington Times Corporation, ©1994.

R eports of psychic phenomena are as old as human history. Experimental tests of psychic phenomena are almost as old. According to Herodotus, the ancient Greek historian, King Croesus of Lydia dispatched several of his men to test seven oracles to see if any of them could divine what he, the king, was doing on the day of the test. Only Pythia, priestess of Apollo at Delphi, was able to divine correctly that the king was making a lamb and tortoise stew in a bronze kettle.

Convinced of her powers, Croesus then posed the question that really interested him: If he attacked the rival kingdom of Persia, would he be able to defeat its army? Pythia replied, "When Croesus has the Halys crossed, a mighty empire will be lost." Insufficiently alert to the ambiguity of this prediction, Croesus crossed the river, attacked, and lost his mighty empire. Evaluating "psychic" data is a risky business.

DEFINITIONS OF PSYCHIC PHENOMENA

The contemporary technical term for psychic phenomena is psi. More precisely, psi denotes anomalous processes of information or energy transfer, processes that are currently unexplained in terms of known physical or biological mechanisms. These processes include *extrasensory perception* (ESP), the acquisition of information without using the known senses, and *psychokinesis*, the ability to affect physical objects or events without the intervention of any known physical force.

In turn, ESP comprises the following:

- *Telepathy.* The transfer of information from one person to another without the mediation of any known channel of sensory communication.
- *Clairvoyance.* The acquisition of information about places, objects, or events without the mediation of any of the known senses (for example, Pythia's knowledge that the king was making stew).
- *Precognition.* The acquisition of information about a future event that could not be anticipated through any known inferential process. (Pythia's prediction about the loss of an empire, although dubious, is an example.)

Serious scholarly investigation of psi began in 1892, when a group of scholars in London founded the Society for Psychical Research (SPR) to

> investigate that large body of debatable phenomena designated by such terms as mesmeric, psychical and spiritualistic . . . without prejudice or prepossession of any kind, and in the same spirit of exact and unimpassioned inquiry which has enabled

Science to solve so many problems, once not less obscure nor less hotly debated.

The SPR was active until the early years of the twentieth century, when many of the original founders had died and enthusiasm declined.

Contemporary psi research is usually considered to have begun in 1927, when Joseph Banks Rhine and his wife/collaborator, Louisa, arrived in the psychology department at Duke University in Durham, North Carolina. Rhine's experiments, which tested for ESP with decks of cards containing geometric symbols, became well known to the general public in 1937 when he published *New Frontiers of the Mind*. The book received widespread press coverage and became a Book of the Month Club selection. Even today, many Americans know of Rhine's work.

Since Rhine, many parapsychologists have reported positive psi results using a wide variety of experimental procedures. Yet most academic psychologists are not yet persuaded that the existence of psi has been established.

SEARCHING FOR A REPEATABLE EXPERIMENT

In science generally, a phenomenon is not considered established until it has been observed repeatedly by several researchers. This criterion has been the source of the most serious criticism of parapsychology: that it has failed to yield a single reliable demonstration of psi that can be replicated by other investigators. In 1974, an experimental procedure was introduced that holds out the promise of supplying that repeatable demonstration: the ganzfeld procedure.

By the late 1960s, several parapsychologists had become dissatisfied with the repetitive forced-choice procedures pioneered by Rhine, believing that they failed to capture the kinds of psi experiences that people report in everyday life. Both historically and cross-culturally, psi has usually been associated with dreaming, meditation, trances of various kinds, and other altered states of consciousness. This suggested that psi information may function like a weak signal normally masked by the sensory "noise" of everyday life. Thus, altered states of consciousness may enhance a person's ability to detect psi information simply because they reduce interfering sensory input. Psi researchers first sought to test this hypothesis by adapting the ganzfeld procedure, a mild sensory isolation technique introduced into experimental psychology during the 1930s.

In a ganzfeld telepathy experiment, one subject (the receiver) rests in a reclining chair in a soundproof chamber. Translucent

Ping-Pong ball halves are taped over the eyes, and headphones are placed over the ears. A red floodlight is directed toward the receiver's eyes, and white noise is played through the headphones. (White noise is a random mixture of sound frequencies similar to the hiss made by a radio tuned between stations.) This homogeneous visual and auditory environment is called the Ganzfeld, a German word meaning "total field." To quiet "noise" produced by internal bodily tension, the receiver is also led through a set of relaxation exercises at the beginning of the ganzfeld period.

THE GANZFELD EXPERIMENT PROVES THE EXISTENCE OF ESP

Most academic psychologists do not yet accept the existence of psi, anomalous processes of information or energy transfer (such as telepathy or other forms of extrasensory perception) that are currently unexplained in terms of known physical or biological mechanisms. We believe that the replication rates and effect sizes achieved by one particular experimental method, the ganzfeld procedure, are now sufficient to warrant bringing this body of data to the attention of the wider psychological community.

Daryl J. Bem and Charles Honorton, *Psychological Bulletin*, vol. 115, no. 1, 1994.

While the receiver is in the ganzfeld, a second subject (the sender) sits in a separate soundproof room and concentrates on the "target," a randomly selected picture or videotaped sequence. For about 30 minutes, the receiver thinks aloud, providing a continuous report of all the thoughts, feelings, and images that pass through his or her mind. At the end of the ganzfeld period, the receiver is presented with several stimuli (usually four) and, without knowing which one was the target, is asked to rate the degree to which each matches the thoughts and images experienced during the ganzfeld period. If the receiver assigns the highest rating to the target, it is scored as a "hit." Thus, if the experiment uses judging sets containing four stimuli (the target and three control stimuli), the hit rate expected by chance is one out of four, or 25 percent.

In 1985 and 1986, the *Journal of Parapsychology* devoted two entire issues to a critical examination of the ganzfeld studies, featuring a debate between Ray Hyman, a cognitive psychologist and a knowledgeable, skeptical critic of parapsychological research, and the late Charles Honorton, a prominent parapsychologist and major ganzfeld researcher. At that time, there had been 42 reported ganzfeld studies conducted by investigators in

10 laboratories.

Across these studies, receivers achieved an average hit rate of about 35 percent. (This might seem like a small margin of success over the 25 percent hit rate expected by chance, but a person with this margin of advantage in a gambling casino would get rich very quickly.) Statistically, this result is highly significant: The odds against getting a 35 percent hit rate across that many studies by chance are greater than a billion to one.

CORRECTING THE FLAWS

If the most frequent criticism of parapsychology is that it has not produced a repeatable psi effect, the second most frequent criticism is that many, if not most, psi experiments have inadequate controls and safeguards. A frequent charge is that positive results emerge primarily from initial, poorly controlled studies and then vanish as better controls and safeguards are introduced.

The potentially most fatal flaws in a psi study are those that would allow a receiver to obtain the target information in normal sensory fashion, either inadvertently or through deliberate cheating. This is called the problem of sensory leakage. Critic Hyman and parapsychologist Honorton agreed that the studies with good safeguards against sensory leakage obtained results that were just as strong as studies that had less good safeguards.

But because Hyman and Honorton disagreed on other aspects of the studies, they issued a joint communiqué in 1986, in which they agreed that the final verdict awaited the outcome of future experiments conducted by a broader range of investigators and according to more stringent standards. They then spelled out in detail the more stringent methodological and statistical standards they believed should govern all future ganzfeld experiments.

In 1983, Honorton and colleagues had initiated a new set of 11 ganzfeld studies that complied with all the guidelines he and Hyman later published in their joint communiqué. They are called autoganzfeld studies because a computer controlled the experimental procedures, including the random selection and presentation of the targets and the recording of the receiver's ratings. These studies were published by Honorton in the *Journal of Parapsychology* in 1990, and the complete history of ganzfeld research was resummarized by Bem (the author of this viewpoint) and Honorton in the January 1994 issue of the *Psychological Bulletin* of the American Psychological Association.

The autoganzfeld studies confirmed the results of the earlier, less sophisticated studies, obtaining virtually the same hit rate:

about 35 percent. These studies also reconfirmed several findings from other research. For example, it has often been reported that creative or artistically gifted persons show high psi ability. The autoganzfeld studies tested this by recruiting twenty students from the Juilliard School in New York City to serve as receivers. Overall, these students achieved a hit rate of 50 percent, one of the highest rates ever reported for a single sample in a ganzfeld study. The autoganzfeld studies also found that significantly higher hit rates were obtained when the targets were videotaped film sequences rather than still pictures.

Even if skeptical critics can agree that the autoganzfeld studies satisfy the strict methodological and statistical criteria set forth in Hyman and Honorton's joint communiqué, the studies cannot, by themselves, satisfy the further requirement that ganzfeld experiments be conducted by a broader range of investigators. In that sense, then, the jury is still out; the verdict awaits the outcome of future experiments. This state of affairs is not likely to change soon.

BELIEF AND SKEPTICISM

The history of science demonstrates that resolving disagreements over the existence of a disputed phenomenon has never been a matter of simply gathering more evidence until it reaches some objective, a priori threshold of quality and quantity. The amount of evidence required to persuade any given scientist that a phenomenon exists depends on his or her belief as to how likely it is that the phenomenon exists in the first place.

Most scientists require more and better evidence for an anomalous phenomenon—one unexplained by known physical and biological mechanisms—than for other phenomena. This is usually expressed by the dictum that "extraordinary claims require extraordinary evidence." But in any given instance, there is no agreement on or objective measure of what constitutes "extraordinary."

Moreover, scientists' diverse reactions to evidence in disputed areas of research are strongly determined by their attitudes toward many other issues, not all of them strictly scientific. For example, scientists differ in the kinds of intellectual risks they are willing to take. For many scientists, it is far more sinful to conclude that an effect exists when it does not than to conclude that an effect does not exist when it does. The choice of which kind of error is more tolerable is not a matter of good science versus bad science but a matter of taste.

As Croesus learned the hard way, evaluating "psychic" data is inherently a risky business.

| "It is too soon for ... 'academic psychologists' to change their minds about psi."

THE EXISTENCE OF ESP HAS NOT BEEN PROVEN

Susan Blackmore

In January 1994, psychologist Daryl J. Bem and parapsychologist Charles Honorton published what they maintain is experimental evidence of the existence of ESP. In the following viewpoint, Susan Blackmore argues that their evidence is unreliable. Bem's and Honorton's analysis, she contends, is based on the faulty research of other parapsychologists. Their results need to be replicated by other researchers before the existence of ESP and other psychic phenomena (psi) can be established, she concludes. Blackmore is a senior lecturer in psychology at the University of the West of England in Bristol, England.

As you read, consider the following questions:
1. What problem did Blackmore find in the ganzfeld experiments set up by Carl Sargent?
2. According to the author, what types of subjects do best in ganzfeld experiments?

From Susan Blackmore, "Psi in Psychology," *Skeptical Inquirer*, Summer 1994. Reprinted by permission of the Committee for the Scientific Investigation of Claims of the Paranormal.

"Most academic psychologists do not yet accept the existence of psi." So begins the abstract of an important paper on parapsychology.

The claim is undoubtedly true, and many will think it ought to stay that way. Yet this quotation implies that the psychologists in question might soon be changing their minds.

It comes, not from a tirade against the skepticism of academia but from an article published in January 1994 in one of psychology's most prestigious academic journals, *Psychological Bulletin*.

Titled "Does Psi Exist? Replicable Evidence for an Anomalous Process of Information Transfer," the article is by parapsychologist Charles Honorton (who died in 1992) and Cornell psychologist Daryl Bem. Bem's high profile and the respect he is accorded by psychologists will ensure that this article is taken seriously and that perhaps some of them will begin to wonder about psi.

So how good is this "replicable evidence"? Is it sufficient, as the authors claim, to suggest the existence of "anomalous processes of information or energy transfer (like telepathy or other forms of extrasensory perception) that are currently unexplained in terms of known physical or biological mechanisms"?

The evidence in question is an overview of research on the ganzfeld. This technique of partial sensory deprivation of subjects in ESP experiments, pioneered by Honorton in the mid-1970s, produced the great Ganzfeld Debate in the mid-1980s, and finally culminated in fully automated testing procedures. The paper reviews the various meta-analyses of ganzfeld findings and, as Honorton has done before, argues that obvious problems like multiple analysis, selective reporting, and methodological flaws cannot be responsible for the high replication rates. It then presents data from "11 new ganzfeld studies."

In 1988 the National Research Council (NRC) produced a report [*Enhancing Human Performance: Issues, Theories, and Techniques,* by Daniel Druckman and John A. Swets, eds.] on enhancing human performance that included a highly negative conclusion on parapsychology. Bem and Honorton have some new light to cast on this report that might seem out of place in an academic article. The NRC apparently solicited a background paper from M.J. Harris and Robert Rosenthal, and this paper noted the impressive ganzfeld results. According to Bem and Honorton, the chair of the NRC committee telephoned Rosenthal and asked him to delete this section of the paper. Rosenthal refused to do so, but the section in question did not appear in the final NRC report.

This is troubling indeed if it means that prejudice is coming before genuine scientific inquiry. It serves more than anything to highlight how difficult it is to stick to purely scientific issues in this controversial area.

Bem and Honorton also accuse the NRC report of not being an independent examination of the ganzfeld because it was heavily based on Ray Hyman's original critique. As for their own paper, I would say it could also be misleading. The strength of some of Hyman's arguments is not at all apparent and the impression is given that many laboratories have found replicable effects.

RELYING ON FLAWED RESEARCH

This claim receives some support from Honorton's analysis, which shows that the overall effect does not depend on just one or two labs. Nevertheless, by far the greatest number of studies were contributed by just two researchers. Out of 28 studies, Honorton contributed 5 and Carl Sargent, at Cambridge, 9. So Sargent's are by far the largest number of studies. However, there were very serious problems with nearly all of Sargent's ganzfeld studies. By failing to mention this, Bem and Honorton imply that these nine studies are reliable research.

The story of my visit to Sargent's laboratory is no secret. I went there to try to find out why Sargent was successful with the ganzfeld while I was not. I observed 13 sessions, of which 6 were direct hits. I then considered whether the hits might be due to sensory leakage, experimental error, fraud, or psi, and made predictions based on all these hypotheses. I was satisfied that sensory leakage was not a problem but found serious errors in the randomization procedure. This cumbersome procedure required sets of sealed, unmarked envelopes containing letters specifying the target selection. On the basis of my various hypotheses I predicted specific errors in the placement and contents of some of these envelopes and, when I was able to open all the envelopes, I found several such errors. I published the findings and Sargent and his colleagues responded, claiming that they were due to minor experimental error.

Whatever one's favored interpretation, it is my opinion that these problems are serious and we should not consider Sargent's studies a valid part of the ganzfeld database. It may be for this reason that parapsychologists now rarely cite them as evidence for psi. So I was disappointed to find that Bem and Honorton did not mention this at all.

BEM AND HONORTON'S "NEW" EXPERIMENTS

They then go on to provide data from "11 new ganzfeld studies." This will perhaps give readers the impression that the data are being presented for the first time. In fact they were previously published, in almost the same form, in the *Journal of Parapsychology* in 1990.

Admittedly they are impressive and deserve presentation to a wider audience than the readers of parapsychology journals. They are the series of experiments using the autoganzfeld—or fully automated ganzfeld system. This was designed to meet the "stringent standards" set by Hyman and Honorton in their joint communique—which ended the great Ganzfeld Debate.

WHY ESP IS STILL CONSIDERED UNPROVEN

Since the beginnings of psychical research in the mid–nineteenth century, its investigators have believed that they have scientific evidence sufficiently strong to place before the general scientific community. Each generation has tried to get the attention of the scientific community with findings that they claim to be irrefutable. The particular evidence put forth has changed from generation to generation. What a previous generation of parapsychologists considered to be a solid case for psi was abandoned by later generations in favor of a more current candidate. This shifting database for parapsychology's best case may be why parapsychology still has not achieved the recognition it desires from the general scientific community.

Ray Hyman, *Psychological Bulletin*, vol. 115, no. 1, 1994.

In this new paper Bem and Honorton claim that these "stringent standards" have been met—a view with which I widely concur. As the experiments are presented here, and in the previous 1990 paper, there are no obvious methodological flaws. The results are highly significant and the effect size is comparable to that found in previous ganzfeld studies. There is also confirmation of findings that emerged from earlier meta-analyses. For example, selected subjects who are artistic and believe in psi do better than unselected subjects. They do better when friends act as senders and dynamic targets are better than static ones.

I think one's response to this should be optimistic. The work so far looks promising—let's see whether the results can be replicated by other researchers.

PROMISING RESEARCH USING AUTOGANZFELD TECHNIQUES

Honorton is no longer with us, but fortunately he was in Edinburgh long enough to help set up the autoganzfeld there for others to continue. In September 1993 the first results were reported at the Society for Psychical Research annual conference in Glasgow.

Two pilot experiments were reported. In the first, 16 unselected subjects, with friends as senders, tried to detect both dynamic and static targets. Results were at chance. In a second study 32 subjects were selected for artistic or musical ability and a positive attitude toward psi. They were tested in pairs using dynamic targets. This time the hit rate was over 40 percent (25 percent is expected by chance), which is comparable to Honorton's previous results.

What can we now conclude? These were only pilot studies carried out by students and they used a ganzfeld setup that was not quite completed. Will these results continue when the promised refinements are in place? Will the final setup really rule out methodological flaws and the chance of experimenter or subject fraud? I await the next set of results with more than bated breath.

In my opinion Bem and Honorton have overstated the strength of the earlier ganzfeld evidence. They have completely ignored the problems with Sargent's work and understated some of Hyman's objections. However, I agree with them that the autoganzfeld procedure appears sound and the results are important. It is too soon for those "academic psychologists" to change their minds about psi, but it is no bad thing that they have been given the chance to consider it.

"The [CIA's remote viewing program's] results appear to provide unequivocal evidence of a human capacity to access events remote in space and time ... by some cognitive process not yet understood."

THE CIA'S REMOTE VIEWING EXPERIMENTS PROVE THE EXISTENCE OF ESP

Harold E. Puthoff

From 1972 to 1995, the CIA and the Department of Defense employed psychics to gather intelligence through remote viewing (the use of psychic ability to locate or describe a far-off target). In the following viewpoint, Harold E. Puthoff describes how the CIA's psi project began and recounts some of the early successes of the remote viewing program. Although the program did not always gather accurate intelligence information, he contends, the overall results of the remote viewing experiments demonstrate that some psychic phenomenon was at work. Puthoff is the former director of the CIA-sponsored remote viewing project at SRI International. He is currently director of the Institute for Advanced Studies at Austin, Texas.

As you read, consider the following questions:

1. According to Puthoff, why was the CIA originally interested in parapsychology research?
2. In the author's opinion, why is it impossible to determine whether information gathered by the remote viewing program influenced policy decisions?

From Harold E. Puthoff, "The CIA & ESP: Taking the Wraps Off Government Remote Viewing Experiments," *Noetic Sciences Review*, Summer 1996. Adapted from the original article, "CIA-Initiated Remote Viewing Program at Stanford Research Institute," *Journal of Scientific Exploration*, vol. 10, no 1, Spring 1996. Reprinted by permission of the author.

W ould phenomena such as remote viewing (RV)—identifying objects not physically at hand—be useful to ensur-
ing "national security"? In July 1995 the US Central Intelligence
Agency (CIA) made its first documented public admission of
significant intelligence community involvement in the psi area.
Although I began this work at Stanford Research Institute (SRI)
in 1972, it was not until 1995 that I found myself for the first
time able to utter in a single sentence the connected initials
CIA/SRI/RV, and to report on some of the early, now declassified, results of what became a multi-year, multi-site, multi-
million-dollar exploration into remote viewing and its possible
"utility for intelligence collection."

BEGINNINGS OF THE RESEARCH

In early 1972 I was involved in laser research at Stanford Research Institute (now called SRI International) in Menlo Park,
California. Ingo Swann—a New York artist who had participated
in many psychic experiments—chanced to see my proposal for
a research project to look into whether physical theory as we
knew it was capable of describing life processes, and suggested
some measurements involving plants and lower organisms. He
wrote me suggesting that if I were interested in investigating the
boundary between the physics of the animate and inanimate, I
should consider experiments of the parapsychological type.

I arranged for access to a well-shielded magnetometer used
in quark-detection experiments in the Physics Department at
Stanford University. During our visit there, sprung as a surprise
to Swann, he appeared to perturb the operation of the magnetometer, located in a heavily shielded vault below the floor of
the building. As if to add insult to injury, he then went on to
"remote view" the interior of the apparatus, rendering by drawing a reasonable facsimile of its rather complex (and heretofore
unpublished) construction. It was this latter feat that impressed
me perhaps even more than the former, as it also eventually did
representatives of the intelligence community. I wrote up these
observations and circulated them among my scientific colleagues in draft form of what was eventually published as part
of a conference proceedings.

THE CIA BECOMES INTERESTED

In a few short weeks a pair of visitors showed up at SRI with the
above report in hand. Their credentials showed them to be from
the CIA. They knew of my previous background as a Naval Intelligence Officer and then civilian employee at the National Secu-

rity Agency several years earlier, and felt they could discuss their concerns with me openly. There was, they told me, increasing concern in the intelligence community about the level of effort in Soviet parapsychology being funded by the Soviet security services. By Western scientific standards, as most working scientists believed, the field of psi research was considered nonsense. As a result the CIA had been on the lookout for a research laboratory outside of academia that could handle a quiet, low-profile classified investigation, and SRI appeared to fit the bill. They asked if I could arrange an opportunity for them to carry out some simple experiments with Swann, and, if the tests proved satisfactory, would I consider a pilot program along these lines? I agreed to consider this, and arranged for the requested tests. (Since the reputation of the intelligence services is mixed among members of the general populace, l have on occasion been challenged as to why I would agree to cooperate with the CIA or other elements of the intelligence community in this work. My answer is simply that as a result of my own previous exposure to this community I became persuaded that war can almost always be traced to a failure in intelligence, and that therefore the strongest weapon for peace is good intelligence.)

The tests were simple, the visitors simply hiding objects in a box and asking Swann to attempt to describe them. The results generated in these experiments are perhaps captured most eloquently by the following example. In one test Swann said, "I see something small, brown and irregular, sort of like a leaf or something that resembles it, except that it seems very much alive, like it's even moving!" The target chosen by one of the visitors turned out to be a small live moth, which indeed did look like a leaf. Although not all responses were quite so precise, nonetheless the integrated results were sufficiently impressive that in short order an eight-month, $49,900 Biofield Measurements Program was negotiated as a pilot study; a colleague, laser physicist Russell Targ, who had a longtime interest and involvement in parapsychology, joined the program; and the experimental effort was begun in earnest.

EARLY REMOTE VIEWING RESULTS

During the eight-month pilot study of remote viewing the effort gradually evolved from the remote viewing of symbols and objects in envelopes and boxes to the remote viewing of local target sites in the San Francisco Bay Area, marked by "beacons," outbound experimenters sent to the site under strict protocols devised to prevent artifactual results. Later judging of the results were similarly handled by double-blind protocols designed to foil artifactual matching.

The CIA contract monitors, ever watchful for possible chicanery, participated as remote viewers themselves in order to critique the protocols. In this role three separate viewers contributed seven of the 55 viewings, several of striking quality.

As summarized in the Executive Summary of the now-released Final Reports of the second year of the program, "The development of this capability at SRI has evolved to the point where visiting CIA personnel with no previous exposure to such concepts have performed well under controlled laboratory conditions (that is, generated target descriptions of sufficiently high quality to permit blind matching of descriptions to targets by independent judges)." What happened next, however, made these results pale in comparison.

LESSONS FROM REMOTE VIEWING RESEARCH

Hundreds of remote viewing experiments were carried out at Stanford Research Institute from 1972 to 1986. The purpose of some of these trials was to elucidate the physical and psychological properties of psi abilities, while others were conducted to provide information for our CIA sponsor about current events in far-off places. We learned that the accuracy and reliability of remote viewing was not in any way affected by distance, size, or electromagnetic shielding, and we discovered that the more exciting or demanding the task, the more likely we were to be successful. Above all, we became utterly convinced of the reality of psi abilities.

Russell Targ, *Noetic Sciences Review*, Summer 1996.

To determine whether it was necessary to have a beacon individual at the target site, Swann suggested carrying out an experiment to remote view the planet Jupiter before the upcoming NASA *Pioneer 10* flyby. In that case, much to his chagrin (and ours) he found a ring around Jupiter, and wondered if perhaps he had remote viewed Saturn by mistake. Our colleagues in astronomy were quite unimpressed as well, until the flyby revealed that an unanticipated ring did in fact exist. (This result was published by us in advance of the ring's discovery.)

Expanding the protocols yet further, Swann proposed a series of experiments in which the target was designated only by geographical coordinates, latitude and longitude in degrees, minutes, and seconds. Needless to say, this proposal seemed even more outrageous than "ordinary" remote viewing.

The remote viewers in the test using these protocols were Ingo Swann and Pat Price, and the entire transcripts are available in the released documents.

Follow-on Programs

By the end of 1975, as a result of the material being generated by both SRI and CIA remote viewers, interest in the program in government circles, especially within the intelligence community, intensified considerably and led to an ever-increasing briefing schedule. This in turn led to an ever-increasing number of clients, contracts and tasking, and therefore expansion of the program to a multi-client base, and eventually to an integrated joint-services program under single-agency (Defense Intelligence Agency) leadership.

In the two decades following 1975 much of the SRI effort was directed less toward developing an operational US capability, but rather toward assessing the threat potential of its use against the US by others. The words "threat assessment" were often used to describe the program's purpose during its development, especially during the early years. As a result much of the remote-viewing activity was carried out under conditions where ground-truth reality could be determined, such as the description of US facilities and technological developments, the timing of rocket test firings and underground nuclear tests, and the location of individuals and mobile units. And, of course, we were responsive to requests to provide assistance during such events as the loss of an airplane or the taking of hostages, relying on the talents of an increasing cadre of remote-viewer/consultants, some well-known in the field, such as Keith Harary, and many who have not surfaced publicly until recently, such as Joe McMoneagle.

Larger Implications

One might ask whether in this program information generated by remote viewing was ever of sufficient significance to influence decisions at a policy level. This is of course impossible to determine unless policy makers were to come forward with a statement in the affirmative. One example of a possible candidate is a study we performed at SRI during the Carter administration debates concerning proposed deployment of the mobile MX missile system. In that scenario missiles were to be randomly shuffled from silo to silo in a silo field, in a form of high-tech shell game. In a computer simulation of a twenty-silo field with randomly assigned (hidden) missile locations, we were able, using remote viewing–generated data, to show rather forcefully that the application of a sophisticated statistical averaging technique (sequential sampling) could in principle permit an adversary to defeat the system.

I briefed these results to the appropriate offices at their request, and a written report with the technical details was widely circulated among groups responsible for threat analysis, and with some impact. What role, if any, our small contribution played in the mix of factors behind the enormously complex decision to cancel the program will probably never be known, and must be considered in all likelihood negligible. This is, however, a prototypical example of the kind of tasking that by its nature potentially had policy implications.

Even though the details of the broad range of experiments, some brilliant successes, many total failures, have not yet been released, we have nonetheless been able to publish summaries of what was learned in these studies about the overall characteristics of remote viewing. Furthermore, over the years we were able to address certain questions of scientific interest in a rigorous way and to publish the results in the open literature.

An unimpassioned observer cannot help but attest to the following fact: Despite the ambiguities inherent in the type of exploration covered in these programs, the integrated results appear to provide unequivocal evidence of a human capacity to access events remote in space and time, however falteringly, by some cognitive process not yet understood. My years of involvement as a research manager in these programs have left me with the conviction that this fact must be taken into account in any attempt to develop an unbiased picture of the structure of reality.

| "The remote viewers did not supply information that was useful in intelligence or other contexts."

THE CIA'S REMOTE VIEWING EXPERIMENTS DO NOT PROVE THE EXISTENCE OF ESP

Ray Hyman

In 1995, the CIA ended a twenty-year remote viewing program that employed psychics to locate or describe secret targets. The CIA concluded that the project did not provide useful intelligence information. In the following viewpoint, Ray Hyman, one of the experts hired by the CIA to evaluate the program, argues that the results of the CIA's remote viewing project do not support the existence of a psychic phenomenon, as proponents of psi claim. In order to prove the existence of psi, he contends, parapsychologists must devise an experiment that consistently demonstrates the phenomenon. Hyman is a psychologist and a professor of psychology at the University of Oregon, Eugene.

As you read, consider the following questions:

1. What were the three components of the Defense Intelligence Agency's Stargate program, according to Hyman?
2. According to the author, what are some of the nonpsychic possibilities that might explain remote viewing "hits"?
3. In the author's opinion, what are the problems created by trying to establish the existence of psi?

From Ray Hyman, "Evaluation of the Military's Twenty-Year Program on Psychic Spying," *Skeptical Inquirer*, March/April 1996. Reprinted by permission of the Committee for the Scientific Investigation of Claims of the Paranormal.

In the early 1970s the Central Intelligence Agency supported a program to see if a form of extrasensory perception (ESP) called "remote viewing" could assist with intelligence gathering. The program consisted of laboratory studies conducted at Stanford Research Institute (SRI) under the direction of Harold Puthoff and Russell Targ. In addition to the laboratory research, psychics were employed to provide information on targets of interest to the intelligence community.

The CIA abandoned this program in the late 1970s because it showed no promise. The Defense Intelligence Agency (DIA) took over the program and continued supporting it until it was suspended in the spring of 1995. Under the DIA the program was named *Stargate* and consisted of three components. One component kept track of what foreign countries were doing in the area of psychic warfare and intelligence gathering. A second component, called the "Operations Program," involved six, and later three, psychics on the government payroll who were available to any government agency that wanted to use their services. The third component was the laboratory research on psychic phenomena first carried out at SRI and later transferred to Science Applications International Corporation (SAIC) in Palo Alto, California.

THE CIA'S EVALUATION OF REMOTE-VIEWING RESEARCH

This program was secret until it was declassified in early 1995. The declassification was done to enable an outside evaluation of the program. Because of some controversies within the program, a Senate committee decided to transfer the program from the DIA back to the CIA. The CIA, before deciding the fate of the program, contracted with the American Institutes for Research (A.I.R.), Washington, D.C., to conduct the evaluation. The A.I.R. hired Jessica Utts, a statistician at the University of California at Davis, and me, a psychologist at the University of Oregon, as the evaluation panel.

The idea was to have a balanced evaluation by hiring an expert who was known to support the reality of psychic phenomena and one who was skeptical about the existence of psi. Utts, in addition to being a highly regarded statistician, has written and argued for the existence of psychic phenomena and has been a consultant to the SRI and SAIC remote-viewing experiments.

Most recently, I served on the National Research Council committee that issued a report stating that the case for psychic phenomena had no scientific justification. In the January 1995 issue of *Psychological Bulletin* I supplied a skeptical commentary on the article by Daryl Bem and Charles Honorton that argued that the recent ganzfeld studies provided evidence for replicable experiments on ESP.

At the beginning of summer 1995, Utts and I were each supplied with copies of all the reports that had been generated by the remote-viewing program during the 20 years of its existence. This consisted of three large cartons of documents.

© 1995 by Herblock in the *Washington Post*.

We met with Edwin May, the principal investigator who took over this remote-viewing research project (after Puthoff and Targ left SRI in the 1980s); representatives of the CIA; and representatives of A.I.R. The purpose of the meeting was to coordinate our efforts as well as to focus our efforts on those remote-viewing studies that offered the most promise of being scientifically respectable. May helped identify the ten best studies for Utts and me to evaluate.

While Utts and I focused on the best laboratory studies, the two psychologists from A.I.R. conducted an evaluation of the recent operational uses of the three remote viewers (psychics) then on the government payroll. We all agreed that any scientifically meaningful evaluation of these operational psychic intelligence uses was impossible. The operational program had been kept separate from the laboratory research, and the work of the remote viewers was conducted in ways that precluded meaningful evaluation. Nevertheless, we all cooperated in developing a structured interview that the A.I.R. staff could use on the program officer, the three psychics, and the individuals or agencies that had used the services of these remote viewers.

The users said, through the interviews, that the remote viewers did not supply information that was useful in intelligence or other contexts.

TYPICAL REMOTE-VIEWING EXPERIMENTS

The remote-viewing experiments that Utts and I evaluated had, for the most part, been conducted since 1986 and presumably had been designed to meet the objections that the National Research Council and other critics had aimed at the remote-viewing experiments conducted before 1986. These experiments varied in a number of ways but the typical experiment had these components:

1. The remote viewers were always selected from a small pool of previously "successful" viewers. May emphasized that, in his opinion, this ability is possessed by approximately one in every 100 persons. Therefore, they used the same set of "gifted" viewers in each experiment.

2. The remote viewer would be isolated with an experimenter in a secure location. At another location, a sender would look at a target that had been randomly chosen from a pool of targets. The targets were usually pictures taken from the *National Geographic*. During the sending period the viewer would describe and draw whatever impressions came to mind. After the session, the viewer's description and a set of five pictures (one of them being the actual target picture) would be given to a judge. The judge would then decide which picture was closest to the viewer's description. If the actual target was judged closest to

the description, this was scored as a "hit."

In this simplified example I have presented, we would expect one hit by chance 20 percent of the time. If a viewer consistently scored more hits than chance, this was taken as evidence for psychic functioning. This description captures the spirit of the experimental evidence although I have simplified matters for convenience of exposition. In fact, the judging was somewhat more complex and involved rank ordering each potential target against the description.

ELIMINATING ALTERNATE EXPLANATIONS OF REMOTE-VIEWING HITS

A hit rate better than the chance baseline of 20 percent can be considered evidence for remote viewing, of course, only if all other nonpsychic possibilities have been eliminated. Obvious nonpsychic possibilities would be inadequacies of the statistical model, inadequacies of the randomization procedure in selecting targets or arranging them for judging, sensory leakage from target to viewer or from target to judge, and a variety of other sources of bias.

The elimination of these sources of above-chance hitting is no easy task. The history of psychical research and parapsychology presents example after example of experiments that were advertised as having eliminated all nonpsychic possibilities and that were discovered by subsequent investigators to have had subtle and unsuspected biases. Often it takes years before the difficulties with a new experimental design or program come to light.

Utts and I submitted separate evaluations. We agreed that the newly unclassified experiments seemed to have eliminated the obvious defects of the earlier remote-viewing experiments. We also agreed that these ten best experiments were producing hit rates consistently above the chance baseline. We further agreed that a serious weakness of this set of studies is the fact that only one judge, the principal investigator, was used in all the remote-viewing experiments. We agreed that these results remain problematical until it can be demonstrated that significant hitting will still occur when independent judges are used.

INCONSISTENCIES BETWEEN CIA RESEARCH AND PSI EXPERIMENTS

Beyond this we disagreed dramatically. Utts concluded that these results, when taken in the context of other contemporary parapsychological experiments—especially the ganzfeld experiments—prove the existence of psychic functioning. I find it bizarre to jump from these cases of statistically significant hitting to the conclusion that a paranormal phenomenon has been proven. As I pointed out, we both agreed that the results of the new remote-viewing experiments have to be independently judged. If independent judges cannot produce the same significant hit rates, this alone would suffice to discard these experiments as evidence of psychic abilities. More to the point, just because these experiments are less than 10 years old and have only recently been opened to public scrutiny, we do not know if they contain hidden and subtle biases or if they can be independently replicated in other laboratories. The history of parapsychology is replete with "successful" experiments that subsequently could not be replicated.

Utts is obviously impressed with consistencies between the new remote-viewing experiments and the current ganzfeld experiments. Where she sees consistencies, I see inconsistencies. The ganzfeld experiments all use the subjects as their own judges. The claim is that the results do not show up when independent judges are used. The exact opposite is true of remote-viewing experiments. When subjects are used as their own judges in remote-viewing experiments, the outcome is rarely, if ever, successful. Successful results come about only when the judges are someone other than the remote viewer. The recent ganzfeld experiments get successful results only with dynamic (animated video clips) rather than static targets. The remote-viewing experiments mostly use static targets. I could go on spelling out such inconsistencies, but this would be futile.

Even if the consistent hit rate above chance can be replicated with independent remote-viewing experiments, this would be a far cry from having demonstrated something paranormal. Parapsychologist John Palmer has argued that the successful demonstration of an above-chance statistical anomaly is insufficient to prove a paranormal cause. This is because remote viewing and ESP are currently only defined negatively. ESP is what is left after the experimenter has eliminated all obvious, normal explanations.

WHAT IS NEEDED TO DEMONSTRATE THAT PSI EXISTS

Several problems are created by trying to establish the existence of a phenomenon on the basis of a negative definition. For one thing, if ESP is shown by any departure from chance that has no obvious normal explanation, there is no way to show that the observed departures are due to one or several causes. Also, the claim for psi can never be falsified, because any glitch in the data can be used as evidence for psi. What is needed, of course, is a positive theory of psychic functioning that enables us to tell when psi is present and when it is absent. As far as I can tell, every other discipline that claims to be a science deals with phenomena whose presence or absence can clearly be decided.

The evidence for N-rays, mitogenetic radiation, polywater, cold fusion, and a host of other "phenomena" that no longer are considered to exist was much clearer and stronger than the current evidence for psychic functioning. In these cases of alleged phenomena, at least we were given criteria to decide when the reputed phenomena were supposed to be present and when they were not. Nothing like this exists in parapsychology. Yet the claim is being made that a phenomenon has been clearly demonstrated.

Fortunately, we do not have to squabble over whether the current remote-viewing experiments do or do not prove the existence of an anomalous phenomenon. We can follow the normal and accepted scientific process of (1) waiting to see if independent laboratories can replicate the above chance hitting conditions using appropriate controls; (2) seeing whether the researchers can devise positive tests to enable us to decide when psi is present and when it is absent; (3) seeing whether they can specify conditions under which we can reliably observe the phenomenon; (4) showing that the phenomenon varies in lawful ways with specifiable variables. Every science—except parapsychology—has met this accepted procedure. So far, parapsychology has not even come close to meeting any of these criteria. It is premature to draw any conclusions. We will simply have to wait and see. If history is a guide, then this will be a long wait, indeed.

> "If a psychic . . . uses his or her position to control people, how awful. If you use it to help, guide, and love people, how great."

PSYCHICS HELP PEOPLE

Mary T. Browne, interviewed by *Psychology Today*

In the following viewpoint, Mary T. Browne describes what she calls her psychic gift and what she believes are visions of the afterlife. She argues that although psychics are not licensed counselors, their advice can help people to come to terms with events in their lives. Browne is a psychic and the author of *Mary T. Reflects on the Other Side: A Compelling Vision of the Afterlife*. She is interviewed here by the editors of *Psychology Today*, a bimonthly magazine.

As you read, consider the following questions:

1. According to Browne, why does she sometimes withhold information from clients?
2. What information should people seek before talking to a psychic, according to Browne?
3. In Browne's opinion, how has the AIDS epidemic affected young people's attitude toward death?

P sychology Today: *How much confidence do you have in your predictions of your clients' futures?*

Mary T. Browne: I am not 100 percent accurate. I don't think anyone really is. But I stand very firm on being accurate a good deal of the time. Even so, I hope people use judgment and weigh the pros and cons when I make a prediction.

Do you ever withhold information?

Yes, I do. When I was younger I may have been too harsh with information. But, after working professionally for 15 years, you learn that certain things will not help the person if said right then. For instance, say someone is very, very upset about her marriage—it is not working at all. She is very unhappy and I see a divorce very clearly. But the client still needs to psychologically work through the problem; she still needs to feel she has done everything humanly possible. So, with information like that, the person needs to go through the steps.

Where does this knowledge come from and how does it come to you?

Sometimes it is images, which is called clairvoyance. When I see people who have died and passed over into the spirit world, it's almost as if they are flashing on a movie screen in front of me. But most of the time the information comes to me in words through my head. It's like turning on a radio. And it comes to me from, I believe, a spiritual place.

A VISION OF HELL

Have you ever been scared by what you saw?

Yes. Through the help of my teacher, Lawrence Hill, I saw the dark side, the realm known as hell. It was a land of no shapes, devoid of love, light, and hope—nothing but the torment of shapeless beings living in their own mistakes. And there was a smell to it. It was a terrible odor psychically, like burning rubber.

What do you say to people who would say that these are the visions of someone who is mentally disturbed? Might a paranoid schizophrenic describe hell the same way or with the same intensity?

Well, if I were sitting on the 57th Street bus and started talking about visions of hell out of the blue, people might think I'm crazy and psychotic, not psychic. I can understand that point of view. But I do come to people with a history. After 15 years and two books, I have shared what I have seen and my life's work. So I think that saves you from a great deal of, "Oh, she's crazy."

What about the psychiatrist who spends 15 years preparing him- or herself to counsel people? Couldn't he or she argue that the psychic doesn't have the equivalent licensing or training?

Everybody should be aware that a psychic is not a licensed

therapist. I find that some clients are so distraught about one thing, that even if you try to move them into the future or the next step, you are pulled right back into this particular issue. It is so involved in their aura that to move on you have to find the reasoning or explanation. Most of it is childhood, so they need the 7,000 hours of therapy, not the hour with the psychic.

So it's a very different service and we don't have the same criteria. That's why people should do their homework before they just talk to a psychic. With the psychiatrist, the American Medical Association does a lot of your homework for you: Doctor So-and-So went to such and such school, has been practicing for 22 years, and here's his diploma. But that doesn't guarantee that your psychiatrist is balanced. In choosing a psychic, you need word of mouth, to read their book, or to talk to a client.

When I went into a trial session with you, you came up with a car accident—the circumstances and color of a car—I had been in. Then you told me about something that had happened to my mother 22 years ago that had changed her whole life. A month later I mentioned it to my mom at the breakfast table. Her coffee cup was literally shaking and she said, "Yes, that's right, and it was exactly 22 years ago." And that was something I didn't know.

Well, I wasn't reading your mind.

That's what I am saying. It is not a part of me, so where does it come from?

Well, it is part of the consciousness and part of the record of your soul development. That's the gift and I gave you verification of it. But I am not a circus performer; I don't do phenomenology by the hour.

The life of a person is quite complex and you can't touch upon everything in an hour. But some images will spiritually or psychically be more important, so they may be shockingly clear or accurate. Hopefully sessions will ultimately help people come to terms with their life and help them deal with what's happening right now.

A RECORD OF PAST LIVES

So do you think that there is a consciousness that we reflect but that we are not aware of ourselves?

There is a record of every single moment of every single life and existence. Think of your physical body as a glove that you take off when you die, but you still have a soul. As a person is reborn with a new body and a new personality, I think we are also reborn with a new memory.

Does anything carry over?

Often you carry over personality tendencies, tests and lessons, and family connections. People are able, now, to have glimpses of things in their past, with proper professional help.

But I think we learn most about our past lives by looking at this one.

Why is it that no one remembers being a schmuck? They were always Napoleon or Peter the Great.

I have a lot of Emily Brontës and Cleopatras. But if you have the personality traits, gifts, and talents of Cleopatra, who brought a country to its knees, I think you are going to have quite a bit of moxie in this life. You are not going to be constantly bombarded with an unsuccessful personal life. But we need to be practical and focus on this life, not the past life, not the next life, not the afterlife. The here and now. Everything we need for our development is here. Yes, there are mysteries and there are people who seek answers in the metaphysical, because the physical does not last.

A PSYCHIC RESPONDS TO SKEPTICS

Mademoiselle: You must come across skeptics a lot. How do you handle them?

Mary T. Browne: If a skeptic sees a miracle, he goes to a doctor to get his eyes checked. All I can say is that I know what I've seen, and I'm obliged to relate that. My main interest is to help people overcome the fear of death and live a happier life. I'm not here to force my ideas on anyone.

Mary T. Browne, interviewed by Valerie Frankel, *Mademoiselle*, August 1994.

You have just written a book about death. It was once a topic nobody wrote about. Now there is a sudden acceptance of the physical reality of death and a spiritual approach to it. What's going on?

I think the AIDS epidemic has opened people up to the discussion of death. When I was younger, I don't remember too many 30-year-olds passing over. We had no epidemic that took the lives of vital, creative young people. Faced with the death of their friends or significant others, people want to understand and explore life and death.

There has also been an opening of a more spiritual discussion of death. It is amazing how many people have had a miraculous experience connected with the death of a family member or loss—like being visited by their father after his death—and how they want to share it.

PSYCHICS AND THE RELIGIOUS COMMUNITY

Do you get any angry calls from priests and rabbis?

Some people sadly have a misconception that a psychic gift is dark. And I think that comes from a gross misunderstanding. It is misunderstood as witchcraft or controlling.

Do they fear that psychics will be confused with religious prophets?

Right, thank you. Religious leaders first tried to stop psychics because they feared they would lose control over people if someone could tell them their future. Those poor people in Salem, I mean, how awful. That was a dark point in history. I don't even like to stop for gas in Salem just because of the vibration.

But Jesus was psychic. He told Thomas, "Before the cock crows, you will betray me three times." Tell me, is that not a psychic prediction?

Yes, but he was extraordinarily well connected.

Well, how nice to have a touch of that—though I am not in any way implying any of us are at that level of development. But I listened to the most psychic man that ever lived. If you are going to walk in his footsteps, my goodness, what a perk to be psychic, too.

But motivation has so much to do with the gift. If a psychic or a religious leader uses his or her position to control people, how awful. If you use it to help, guide, and love people, how great. It is the motive behind the deed.

How important was growing up in Iowa, an agrarian society, in your life? Did it have anything to do with how you look at growth and death and cycling?

I am very grateful for Iowa. It is the basis for my emotional balance. I think Midwesterners are wonderful people. They are open, loving, pragmatic, and believe in afterlife and spirituality. My grandma Grace raised me with the tools to trust my judgment, to respect a gift, not to go loony-tunes about it.

Common sense reigned there. I think a lot of life's problems that people think are psychological or spiritual are really just common sense.

People worry too much, instead of taking action. They think too much about themselves and not the needs of others. But it is all basically a process of growth. That's why we are born, that's why we live on this side, then go to the other side, and come back until we do it right.

Life is all about getting it right and we get it right when we master ourselves.

> "There seems to be one characteristic common to all oracles: They take little responsibility for the accuracy of their advice."

PSYCHICS HARM PEOPLE

Mark Matousek

In the following viewpoint, Mark Matousek, a contributing editor for *Common Boundary* and author of *Sex, Death, Enlightenment: A True Story*, describes some harmful experiences that he and his acquaintances have had with psychics. He argues that advice given by psychics often harms people by keeping them from dealing with specific problems in a direct, effective manner.

As you read, consider the following questions:

1. According to Matousek, why are people "flocking" to psychic oracles?
2. In the author's opinion, why is the practice of offering generic advice to people with specific problems "insidious"?

From Mark Matousek, "Painting Devils," *Common Boundary*, March/April 1996. Reprinted by permission of the author.

M y sister-in-law was telling me the other day about how her Turkish grandmother used to read coffee grounds to predict the future.

"This old lady would be sitting there at the kitchen table, pushing her finger around the bottom of a cup, trying to get me to sit down for a reading," Cali said, rolling her eyes. "For years I used to say to her, 'Nona, please leave me alone. I don't want to know the future. What's the point? It'll be bad enough when it happens.'"

I understand what Cali means. I'm not as pessimistic as she is, thank God, but I am a great believer in focusing on the present moment and not getting lost in occult speculation. It worries me that people nowadays may be flocking to oracles (an umbrella term I'm using, for the sake of argument, to include anyone who claims to predict the future) out of rank terror or idle curiosity. It worries me that they may be using oracles to counter anxiety, to stuff the void of being here now, to whitewash their perfectly human frustration at having only five (usable) senses in a multisensory dimension. These strategies worry me not because there's anything inherently harmful in psychic guidance, but because these seers may be profiting from our terror, diverting us from the challenge of living in beginner's mind. What exactly is the wisdom of trying to know the future, I ask myself. Isn't it hard enough to deal with what *is*? Isn't the overweening urge to know more than you're meant to a sort of hubris?

AN EXPERIENCE WITH ASTROLOGY

I speak from some experience. A couple of years ago, I accepted an offer to have my astrological chart done. Until then, I'd always resisted psychic aid, had been almost fanatically opposed to all forms of what I considered magical dabbling But sometimes I need to challenge my own prejudices, so I agreed to the reading. The astrologer was an editor I liked (I like any editor who returns my phone calls and doesn't screw up my copy); he was also, by reputation, an expert in the ways of the stars, having completed a 10-year study of the subject. Finally, he was someone I'd never met and probably never would, thus assuring my skeptical mind that the information he'd give me would be based solely on my horoscope.

When the morning of our phone date came, I called him in Illinois. For the next hour, he talked to me about the tilting constellations—transits, cusps, and retrogrades—describing what he believed these astral bodies light-years away seemed to be saying about my little life. Mostly, his predictions were sunny, though I noticed that he steered away from details and specifics. His only darker warning was this: to beware of the following spring, when my health would be in danger.

I tried to shrug his words off with the cliché that astrology deals in probabilities, not absolutes. However, with the seed of apprehension planted, I couldn't forget the prophecy. As March approached, I started to worry. Through April, May, and most of June, calamity hovered in the back of my brain. Not until July had come and gone and spring was safely behind me was I able to relax completely and forget the astrologer's onus.

Bizarro by Dan Piraro is reprinted courtesy of Chronicle Features Syndicate, San Francisco, California. All rights reserved.

Afterward, I asked myself what I had accomplished by pushing my instincts aside and venturing into the Oracle Zone. The answer was: nothing at all, except to add stress to my already combustible life. I thought of the Finnish saying that warns us not to "paint devils on the wall," not to conjure more problems than we already have. It could be argued that the astrologer's warning prompted me to take better care of myself that spring than I might have otherwise, but that's speculation. The truth (according to me) is that this proliferating oracle business is truly questionable, as most spiritual teachers will attest. Not one enlightened person I know of recommends the magical arts as a hobby, or a crutch, not only because personal power of the kind oracles offer is dangerous if misused, but because the individuals peddling this service are frequently wrong.

Psychics Do Not Take Responsibility

The question of legitimacy among oracles is too complex to tackle here, though it seems likely that for every bona fide psychic there are at least three amateurs profiting from the public's gullibility. These seers read everything from tarot cards to horoscopes, runes, palms, and auras. They work on the Internet, in bus stations, at New Age centers, and in chic storefronts in Greenwich Village. Some are trained in long traditions of occult arts; others make it up as they go along. Yet for all their diversity, there seems to be one characteristic common to all oracles: They take little responsibility for the accuracy of their advice. Hiding behind a sort of mystical disclaimer that says, "Hey, I'm only guessing," they leave themselves free to make predictions for profit without personal liability. Imagine an M.D. who could treat you this way—"Well, Mrs. Smith, it might be cancer or it might be gas. We'll wait and see if the groundhog sees its shadow."

This sounds absurd, but I've known my share of psychic casualties. I've watched intelligent people turn gaga in the presence of supposed oracles. A few years ago, an otherwise brilliant, politically active liberal I know actually followed his psychic teacher's brainstorm that everyone should buy Krugerrands while apartheid was still being practiced in South Africa. When I asked him how he could possibly be so naive, he shrugged and said that he figured his teacher knew something he didn't. Another was advised, during his father's final illness, to cut off all contact with his family and not to attend his father's funeral. Someone else was told by a psychic that he was about to embark on the most important love affair of his life, then had his bones jumped by that same wacko, who admitted afterward that his prediction had been a setup. Aside from this sort of flagrant misdirection, there is the more common but equally insidious practice of offering generic advice on specific problems—elliptical messages open to multiple interpretations, which often confuse people in need of genuine guidance.

PSYCHICS DO NOT RELATE BAD NEWS

Many of my best friends disagree with me. They think that I'm afraid of expanding my mind and relinquishing autonomy. (They're partially right on that score.) They call me a spiritual reactionary and return with glowing reports of their encounters with oracles around the globe, full of adjectives like "uncanny." When my eyebrow sneaks up, they tell me that I'm an awful pessimist, that most psychics mean well, work with compassion, and struggle to be as accurate as possible. Though immune to the rigors of malpractice, oracles, I'm assured, do aspire to a central tenet of the Hippocratic oath: to do no harm if they can help it. Other than the sort of vague warning I received from the astrologer in Illinois, my friend Robert maintains, oracles are honor-bound not to tell you anything really scary. "Even if they see bad things, they only tell you what can be useful," he says.

What I want to know is: Who is the oracle to decide for me what's useful and what isn't? Even though I'm not looking for bad news, how could I trust somebody who withheld it? Beyond that, what role might self-interest play in this censorship? How popular would a psychic be if he told his clients the whole truth? Not extremely, I suspect, but I'd still prefer the plain facts to a prophecy that has been parsed to please me.

I feel like such a Scrooge when I grouse this way. What's wrong with being supported, affirmed, encouraged through life's uncertainties by confirmation from the great beyond? What's wrong with gathering information, taking what's useful, and leaving the rest? We're adults who can discriminate, right? I'm really not so sure. A true believer I know who swears by his astrologer (though the predicted movie deal with Steven Spielberg hasn't quite materialized) was recently told that he shouldn't even bother pursuing romance this year. Rather than being discouraged by the disturbing news that love was not in the stars for '96, my unhappy-to-be-a-bachelor friend appeared relieved.

"Why are you so happy?" I asked him.

"'Cause now I know it's not my fault."

"It's not?"

"No. It's just not in the stars."

PSYCHICS VS. FREE WILL

I find this so distressing. Of course, I'm glad that my friend's self-blame is momentarily softened, glad that his loneliness has been appeased by explanation. But what does his reaction to the astrologer's prognosis say about free will? What does it say about the desire, shared by nearly everyone, to give ourselves over to magical authority, to shake free the burden of self-determination? Isn't it dangerous to accept a stranger's word on something as important as one's love life, to shut down the aspiration that magnetizes our hearts' desires and to risk fulfilling the oracle's prophecy?

We're highly impressionable beings, after all, confused by tumbling circumstance, often more needy for guidance than we'd ever admit. When that guidance comes from psychic authority, it tends to assume a greater legitimacy, which is why the potential for spiritual abuse is always so great. What I want to say to my bachelor friend is that although I'm glad he's feeling better, I'm troubled by his eagerness to shrug off the complexity of his life on the basis of a hundred-dollar phone call. "Forget the constellations!" I want to shout. "Get off Uranus and figure out once and for all why you keep chasing your lovers away!"

I never would, though. It's none of my business. Life's tough for everyone, the mystery too much to live with sometimes. The suspense of waiting for Godot is frequently unbearable, I know, but to me that's the thrill of it. I'm a sucker for surprise. The day-to-day expectation of never knowing what's ahead is exhilarating to me; it keeps me on my toes, keeps me in the present tense. I have no desire to play leapfrog with time. It's all I can do, on a good day, to make sense of what's right in front of me.

Like my sister-in-law waving away her coffee-slinging grandma, I say to the oracles who come my way, "Thanks, but no thanks. The future will be here soon enough."

PERIODICAL BIBLIOGRAPHY

The following articles have been selected to supplement the diverse views presented in this chapter. Addresses are provided for periodicals not indexed in the *Readers' Guide to Periodical Literature*, the *Alternative Press Index*, the *Social Sciences Index*, or the *Index to Legal Periodicals and Books*.

Julie Baumgold	"When You Gotta Have Friends," *Esquire*, October 1994.
Jayne M. Blanchard	"Marketing the Sixth Sense," *Common Boundary*, November/December 1994. Available from 5272 River Rd., Suite 650, Bethesda, MD 20816.
Larry Dossey	"The Science of Prayer," *Natural Health*, March/April 1994. Available from 17 Station St., Brookline Village, MA 02147.
Valerie Frankel	"After Death, What?" *Mademoiselle*, August 1994.
Ray Hyman	"The Evidence for Psychic Functioning: Claims vs. Reality," *Skeptical Inquirer*, March/April 1996.
Jeffrey Kluger	"CIA ESP," *Discover*, April 1996.
Marci McDonald	"Telling Fortunes," *Maclean's*, September 4, 1995.
Jill Neimark	"Do the Spirits Move You?" *Psychology Today*, September/October 1996.
Rupert Sheldrake	"Telepathic Pets," *New Age Journal*, September 1995. Available from 42 Pleasant St., Watertown, MA 02172.
Gordon Stein	"Mediumship: Is It Mixed or Just Mixed Up?" *Skeptical Inquirer*, May/June 1995.
Melissa Townsend	"How I Found My Psychic Gift," *Mademoiselle*, April 1994.
Gregory Vistica	"Psychics and Spooks," *Newsweek*, December 11, 1995.
Douglas Waller	"The Vision Thing," *Time*, December 11, 1995.
Linton Weeks	"Up Close and Personal with a Remote Viewer," *Washington Post*, December 4, 1995.

CHAPTER 4

DOES LIFE AFTER DEATH EXIST?

CHAPTER PREFACE

With modern advances in emergency life-saving procedures, many people who clinically "die" are resuscitated. A few of those who have died and lived to tell about it have described strange and remarkable near-death experiences (NDEs). The typical NDE, as reported by experiencers, involves traveling through a tunnel toward a bright light, feeling warm and peaceful, and encountering a deceased relative or some "being of light" who reassures the experiencer and tells him or her to return to life. Many of those who return to life believe that they have had a glimpse of the afterlife and feel spiritually transformed by the experience.

Raymond Moody is the author of *Life After Life*, the 1975 book that pioneered the field of NDE studies. Having studied the phenomenon for more than twenty years, he is convinced that the reports of near-death experiencers are proof that life after death exists. According to Moody, those who have been revived are invariably happier, more confident, more at peace, and better able to grapple with unpleasant aspects of life. "That NDEs totally transform those who experience them demonstrates their reality and power," he asserts.

But others remain skeptical of the veracity of near-death experiencers and of the accuracy of accounts of the afterlife. Maurice Rawlings, author of *To Hell and Back*, calls the spiritual transformations of near-death experiencers the "religion of the resuscitated." It is not surprising, he maintains, that those who are given a second chance at life are nicer and happier than they were before. Douglas Groothuis, assistant professor of religion and ethics at Denver Seminary, is the author of *Deceived by the Light*. He warns that "those returning from near-death may have clinically died, but they have not . . . been resurrected." In his opinion, it is unwarranted to credit the visions of near-death experiencers as true descriptions of the afterlife.

Since the advent of medical methods of resuscitating clinically dead patients, researchers have been looking for ways to scientifically prove that life after death exists. The viewpoints in the following chapter debate whether NDEs and past-life memories provide proof of life after death.

| "Such a kaleidoscope of [near-death] experience MUST represent something that is indisputably real."

NEAR-DEATH EXPERIENCES ARE VISIONS OF THE AFTERLIFE

Beverly C. Jaegers

With advances in medical technology, many people have survived medical emergencies in which they have come very close to dying. Some of these people report that while they were "dead" they saw a tunnel leading to a bright light. In the following viewpoint, Beverly C. Jaegers argues that the similarity of details in accounts of near-death experiences (NDEs) proves that survivors are all experiencing the same phenomenon—namely, visions of the afterlife. She maintains that skeptical researchers have not been able to replicate the NDE through brain stimulation or drugs. Jaegers is a psychic and the leader of the United States Psi Squad, a psychic investigation group that assists police investigations.

As you read, consider the following questions:

1. What are some common elements of near-death experiences listed by Jaegers?
2. According to the author's estimate, how many people have had an NDE?
3. Why does brain stimulation fall short as an explanation for NDE, in the author's opinion?

From Beverly C. Jaegers, *The Doorway to Forever* (St. Louis: Mind Development Control Association, 1994). Copyright ©1994, Beverly C. Jaegers. Reprinted by permission of the author and the author's agent, The Pimlico Agency, Inc.

The scene is familiar to medical people in hospitals or emergency service units. A man or woman is near death, apparently unaware of all surroundings or stimuli, when suddenly, his or her face brightens, a tremulous smile may appear, and with open eyes, a look of surprise suffuses the face. Seconds later, the life is gone, forever. . . .

What is this surprise that is seen on most faces of those who were conscious or semiconscious at death? Have they seen or heard something for which they were not prepared?

For the answers, we must go to the typical experience of those who have walked beyond the barrier of death, and then returned from it . . . the experience known as the Near-Death Experience or NDE.

These episodes are found in wide varieties, but they also share a common thread, and many of the scenes described are so heartbreakingly similar that they leave no question that the experience was a true one. Commonalities include the light, a tunnel, a canopy, "being at the bottom of an open grave," an urge to follow the brilliant light, being told to return to one's body, and a wide variety of other similarities.

ASHLEY'S NEAR-DEATH EXPERIENCE

Recently, a child of five, the only survivor of a deadly accident caused by a drunk driver in outstate Missouri, awakened from a 16-day coma on Easter Sunday. She related to her grandparents and nurses, who were reluctant to tell her that she had lost her mother and brother, that she had just been with these people while in the period of unconsciousness. Her head injuries were grievous and during the first hours after the wreck, she'd apparently died, medically. She retained a clear memory of the event, telling all who would listen that she had met her mother and brother being led away, hand in hand, by a male figure. She said that he looked like "Santa Claus," and that he had told her not to follow but to go back alone. Her mother had told her that she loved her deeply, as had her young brother, and the two had told her goodbye. As she told this, it confirmed what those around her had seen when the child awakened from the coma. Upon awakening, Ashley had immediately turned her head to the hospital room's wall, and in a soft voice, began talking with someone who wasn't visibly there. She smiled, waved and said, "I love you, Mom, I love you, Daniel. Bye-bye."

Ashley says that there were "a lot of people" there "that day" when her mother and brother died. She wanted to go with them, but the man with a mustache told her that she could not.

Who was the "man with a mustache" and why did she relate him to Santa Claus?

The three drunks were killed in the head-on crash, as well as another woman and her child, in addition to Ashley's mother and eleven-month-old brother. It would seem that there were indeed "a lot of people" there, all going somewhere, but only Ashley was told not to come along.

This girl had never heard of a "typical NDE," had no special religious programming, and certainly did not know, at that time, that her mother and sibling had died while she remained alive. Who can doubt the truth expressed by a child who knows what she experienced and can describe it in detail; she knows what she saw.

COMMON ELEMENTS OF NEAR-DEATH EXPERIENCES

Other people of all ages in accidents and trauma have experienced the exact same thing, with perhaps some details Ashley didn't notice. Many report a dark tunnel leading to light. Many just describe the brilliance of a tremendous light which bathes everything in its radiance. Some have reported little "sparkles" in this light, moving and twirling around.

So is the gateway to our afterlife really something like the final scene in the movie Ghost? All of these elements were there, plus the suggestion of a crowd of robed misty figures at the other end of the tunnel or roadway of light.

These correlations and so-called "coincidences" in what happened to persons who briefly experienced death before being returned to life were formerly written off by the medical profession to be carbon dioxide overload, which could induce the hallucination of being sucked down a tunnel. Many patients undergoing an NDE have normal oxygen levels both before and after. And the tunnel is only part of the experience.

In actual fact, this experience has been described after near-death for hundreds, perhaps thousands, of years and in all languages of mankind. Only recently have any attempts been undertaken to study or to understand the NDE and its effect on the life of the individual who has undergone it.

In the Missouri-Illinois area, there is perhaps no more well-known name than Peggy Raso of the International Association for Near-Death Studies (IANDS). This is a group formed to inform, not just to record, these happenings, although that is one of its functions. Peggy is a "NDE-er" herself and underwent her own experience following childbirth. She was stymied until she heard some IANDS researchers being interviewed on the radio and realized that there was some investigation going on and that many thousands of people have had an NDE. In fact, a recent poll indicates that as many as 13 million have admitted having this experience or one so similar they cannot be considered as anything else!

Although this phenomenon had been occurring for such a long time, it was not scientifically studied until the interest of such researchers as Dr. Ian Stevenson at the University of Virginia was sparked. In fact, Peggy herself was sent to a psychiatrist after her experience, and there was much snickering and many "suggestions" to "talk to Dr. Stevenson" which she now wishes she had followed up.

MEETING SPIRITS IN THE AFTERLIFE

In the process of researching my book Life After Life, I discovered that people who have near-death experiences also report encounters with a form of apparition. As they enter into a realm of light, they are met by the spirits of relatives and friends who have previously died. These experiences are often transformative, frequently having positive aftereffects.

Raymond Moody, New Age Journal, November/December 1993.

The work of pioneer researchers such as Dr. Stevenson, Dr. Raymond Moody, Dr. Bruce Greyson and Dr. Kenneth Ring, Ph.D., has led to the present establishment of IANDS studies at the University of Connecticut, where serious research has been done since its initiation in 1981.

Following her discovery of Kenneth Ring on KMOX radio, talking about his book Going Toward Omega, Peggy wrote him about her own experience. At that time, there was no formal association of NDE-ers, per se, but from such letters came the formation of the research group which exists today. . . .

A MILLION NEAR-DEATH EXPERIENCERS CANNOT BE WRONG

What are we to imply from today's millions who have admittedly had a near-death experience in comparison with the less well documented thousands who had them in earlier centuries? Perhaps the proliferation is due to the existence of better medical emergency services, thus saving many patients who would have died only a few years ago. Certainly we can draw no religious significance from it, as experiences are had by persons of all persuasions, in all countries of the world, and who speak a bewilderingly wide range of languages—all repeating the same words.

Such a kaleidoscope of experience MUST represent something that is indisputably real, not just real to the beholder. Tiny children have had the experience, relating it without the prejudice of ingrained fear of criticism. Ordinary people struck down suddenly in the midst of their ordinary daily activities have detailed their near-death experience to emergency medical service (EMS) workers, emergency room nurses and doctors, critical care personnel, and to everyone else who would listen. Grudgingly, slowly, acceptance is coming that there is definitely something beyond the supposed "end" called death. There is a doorway of some sort . . . a doorway to forever. . . .

A TIME TO DIE

There must be, and apparently is, a "time" when we aren't "supposed" to die. If not, we would be sadly lacking in first-person NDEs such as those that fill contemporary books. Is it true that there is indeed *a time to live and a time to die?* There seems no other reason for the NDE—these individuals are not yet at the end of their allotted span.

In my own files is an experience where a woman of great intellect, a law professor and social leader, was felled by an unexpected heart attack. Metaphysically aware, this woman had met and spoken with several who had experienced the NDE. However, this time it was her own life in the balance. Brought back by physicians from the misty tunnel and the light beyond, she was not grateful but extremely angry! Her husband had died years before, and she thought she'd seen him in the misty light. She felt peace, heard music and smelt roses (a special flower symbol for her) while in this "other" place. She wanted to stay, yet was yanked back by the ministrations of emergency room personnel. It made her mad.

She related this to another of my group who was visiting her in the hospital three days later. She had experience with the death experience and had tasted the peace and joy of the life beyond. Her anger was at being forced medically to leave all this, for she knew her job was done on Earth and it was time to go.

Jane had another heart attack only a few hours later, and this time they let her go. We know that she is now with her husband and is at peace.

But what of those who have not yet finished their jobs here, or who have not reached that "time to die"?

Peggy Raso tells me that most give the reason that they were told to return. It is not often that a reason for this is given, and the overwhelmingly most common reason is that there are earthly tasks not yet completed. Many times it is that there are children yet to raise, other times another type of task that is undone.

EXPERIENCERS GIVEN A MISSION TO TEACH

We learned from Earl Poese of St. Charles, Missouri, that he was told to return and to witness to the reality of his religion and to that of psychic healing and prayer healing. Earl has long taught these realities, although he was unlettered before his NDE and had never taught a class in any subject. Although a kind and gentle man, he had ordinary religious feelings and no special "calling" to teach or to exhibit religion. He was told by one of the beings he met in the beyond that this would be his mission.

As a teacher myself, of ESP and other things, I know just how hard and thankless a job it can be to teach adults. Teaching young children was a breeze compared to that. Yet Earl was told to begin a new career, in effect, in his later sixties, and to teach adults about the reality of God and healing. Wow!—what a plateful that was! And yet he has taken it on, and even now, a dozen years later, is still at it and has had no further severe heart problems. This man was given a mission—a challenge.

Other persons who have had NDEs have been told to return, yet given no specific mission. Many of them have become teachers on a lesser level, however, merely by sharing their experience. A mission, yes, but not a formal one.

Usually the NDE leaves a man or woman with a sense of peace, a surety of life beyond life, a strong sense of enjoyment in the fruits and comforts of daily existence in this world. Perhaps they also teach this in their example to us.

Yet others are given a specific task to do, and usually this is involved on one level or another with healing, comforting and helping others to reach their own highest spiritual awareness. . . .

DRUG AND BRAIN STIMULATION RESEARCH

Those who still question the reality of the NDE are seemingly gratified that some brain researchers have been able to stimulate such a visual phenomena by touching a specific portion of the brain located just above the ear. Lights are seen, and feelings of "otherworldliness" are initiated. They actually think that they, in their scientific way, have found the reason for the NDE. Others, studying drug side-effects, have postulated that morphine or other hypnotic drugs are responsible for this mind experience (hallucinations, no less).

This set of explanations is falling far short of the reality and power of the true NDE. First, the brain-stimulators have not and cannot produce the real tunnel, the real light, and the other events which make up the ordinary NDE. In not one case has a patient undergoing this form of experimental brain stimulation encountered a "presence," relative or loved one. Not a single one of their guinea pigs has reported being spoken to or being told that they must not stay there, nor given any reasons why they should leave. This stimulated experience is as much a counterfeit as a laser copy of the Mona Lisa!

The second reason given, drugs to kill pain, falls far short of the truth as well. No such phenomena were ever reported previous to the emergence of the NDE as an actual and common experience for the dying. Until quite recently, in fact, no one cared to share their NDE, as they were certain that it would be laughed at or, at the very least, misunderstood. In other words, this is a half-baked guess on someone's part, the sort of guess that becomes a rumor and with enough repetition, a truth. But it is not truth. In my own extensive study of such drugs as morphine, thorazine, codeine, opium, etc., I can find no recorded side-effect of this sort, nor can they.

THERE WILL ALWAYS BE SKEPTICS

Finally, we must consider that no matter what the phenomenon, there is always a Greek chorus of naysayers who would refuse to believe such things happened even if they were the ones to whom it happened. Or as my grandfather used to say, they wouldn't know a fact if it was wrapped around their ankles!

Why scientific education should have led to bigoted rejection of all so-called spiritual events it is hard to say. Got an answer? If so, tell me.

> "The [near-death experience] stories
> are a veritable twilight zone of
> inconsistencies."

NEAR-DEATH EXPERIENCES ARE NOT VISIONS OF AN AFTERLIFE

Roy Rivenburg

Those who believe near-death experiences (NDEs) are visions of the afterlife argue that the similarity of the reported experiences prove NDEs are real. In the following viewpoint, Roy Rivenburg, a staff writer with the *Los Angeles Times*, reports that there are actually many striking discrepancies between various near-death accounts. Furthermore, he notes, visions similar to NDE accounts have been produced in laboratory experiments using electrical brain stimulation or drugs. These findings, Rivenburg writes, have led skeptical researchers to discount NDEs as hallucinations.

As you read, consider the following questions:

1. How does Kenneth Ring, cited by Rivenburg, reconcile the differences in reports of the afterlife?
2. How does Douglas Lyle, quoted by the author, explain incidents where people report events that occurred while they were "dead"?
3. According to Melvin Morse, quoted in the viewpoint, what is the role of the brain's right temporal lobe?

Lightning shot through the telephone and into Dannion Brinkley's body, welding the nails in his shoes to the nails in the floor—and sending his soul on one of the most bizarre near-death sojourns ever recounted.

According to his best-selling book, *Saved by the Light*, Brinkley traveled to a luminous crystal city where he met 13 silver-blue spirit beings, learned of calamities in store for the Earth and saw his entire life flash before him.

Or so the story goes.

For decades, Americans have been mesmerized by the tales of modern-day Lazaruses like Brinkley. They've bought millions of books about the afterlife, watched a litany of the ex-dead on talk shows, and devoured countless back-from-beyond tales in the media.

Some are so eager to hear about the hereafter that they seem to be blinded by the light. Despite the best shots from critics, they still give the benefit of the doubt. Even when things seem doubtful indeed.

Brinkley says his life review covered "at least 6,000 fistfights" that he had between fifth and 12th grades. That averages out to two brawls a day, nonstop for eight years, making Brinkley the Wilt Chamberlain of schoolyard pugilism.

He also says he was a Marine Corps sniper during the Vietnam War, dispatched to Cambodia and Laos to assassinate enemy officers and politicians. But military records show that Pfc. Brinkley was never a sniper, never saw combat, indeed never left the United States during his 18 months in the service.

He was a truck driver stationed in Atlanta.

Brinkley declines to offer any evidence of overseas duty, saying the government is covering up his record because it is classified. But several sources inside and outside the military (including ex-Marines involved in the same covert operations Brinkley claims a role in) say his tale is full of holes and that the so-called secret files are all public.

But his story isn't the first to be challenged.

REMARKABLE INCONSISTENCY OF NEAR-DEATH STORIES

Ever since Dr. Raymond Moody, a psychiatrist, coined the term "near-death experience" in 1975, the popular assumption has been that all such reports are remarkably similar and provide startling evidence for a hereafter.

Scratch beneath those flat EKG lines, however, and the stories are a veritable twilight zone of inconsistencies. Some near-death voyagers claim to have met God—but a few saw Elvis or Groucho Marx, researchers say. Others get to heaven not through the famous "tunnel" but aboard ghostly taxicabs, ferries that cross the River Styx, or spangled cows.

Even children—often touted as the best source of unbiased information—commonly return from "death" claiming they were greeted in the other world by living teachers and Nintendo characters instead of deceased relatives.

There also have been psychic slip-ups. In the late 1970s and early '80s, for instance, re-mortalized adults around the globe kept telling researchers of divinely inspired forecasts of a coming apocalypse. The near-unanimous date: 1988. . . .

HARD-TO-EXPLAIN DIFFERENCES

If people actually are entering another dimension, write parapsychology researchers Karlis Osis and Erlandur Haraldsson, "we should expect all patients to see essentially the same thing."

To be sure, there are some striking similarities. Beings of white light, feelings of peace, and indescribable colors and sights ("the world split . . . [and] everything was silver . . . like diamonds and stars") turn up repeatedly.

Many also report strange buzzing sounds, aerial views of their lifeless bodies and eerie replays of their entire past, like "images from film sprung loose in a projector."

But there also are some hard-to-explain differences, Dr. Melvin Morse, a Seattle pediatrician and near-death researcher, says.

Whereas American near-death survivors are typically sent back by God because "it's not your time yet," India's afterlife visitors are more likely to be told there was a "clerical error."

The terrain of heaven also varies wildly—from gardens, forests or cattle-filled pastures in some accounts to clouds, computer rooms or castles in others. A Texan saw barbed-wire fences in the afterlife; Micronesians describe large, noisy cities with cars and skyscrapers.

Kenneth Ring, professor emeritus of psychology at the University of Connecticut and a co-founder of the International Assn. for Near-Death Studies, reconciles the contradictions by suggesting that the next world has as many topographies as this one, and that departed souls enter it at different locations. Others argue that the spiritual realm simply defies description, forcing visitors to fall back on words that reflect their culture or upbringing.

But the discrepancies don't end with physical layouts. The very nature of the afterlife has been drastically altered in recent years.

"Gone are the bad deaths, harsh judgment scenes, purgatorial torments and infernal terrors of medieval [near-death records]," writes Carol Zaleski in *Otherworld Journeys*, a comparison of modern and ancient post-mortem visions. "In today's upbeat near-death literature . . . the being of light communicates, but never excommunicates."

REPORTS OF ELVIS SIGHTINGS

Even more curious: Sometimes the being of light is Elvis.

Moody has chronicled at least two such sightings. In one, a Nebraska teacher who had met the singer briefly in real life encountered him again when her heart stopped during gallbladder surgery in 1979. "Hi, Beverly, remember me?" the slimmed-down King reportedly asked as he stepped from the light.

But Ring says it's unfair to take "the most extreme, exotic cases . . . and use them to cast doubt on the rest [because] 98% of near-death visions really [are] similar."

Morse, on the other hand, insists that near-death visions are "very dissimilar . . . very idiosyncratic."

Backing up that view is Zaleski, a Smith College religion professor whose research in the field is widely regarded as among the most thorough and objective.

Considered closely, she writes, the similarities between modern and medieval afterlife stories are impressive—but so are the differences, so much so that "we can no longer insist that [near-death visions] paint a true picture of what occurs at the [end] of life."

But believers are not easily dissuaded. They reel off story after story of mysterious psychic phenomena and electrical disturbances said to accompany the near-death experience. Could a mere hallucination cause that? they ask.

For instance, Atlanta cardiologist and near-death author Michael Sabom says patients who report out-of-body journeys were able to accurately describe conversations and medical procedures that took place during their "deaths."

Such incidents can seem spooky, says Dr. Douglas Lyle, a Laguna Hills, California, cardiologist. But there is a possible physiological explanation: "The brain is obviously still alive and receiving [sensory] input" after the heart has stopped. "It's kind of like someone sending you e-mail when your computer is off and you don't know it's there until you turn it on."

ANECDOTAL EVIDENCE OF NEAR-DEATH EXPERIENCES

Other near-death tales seem harder to dismiss, such as the Hartford Hospital patient who reportedly saw a red shoe on the roof (a janitor later retrieved it), or the blind person who supposedly described colors and other visual details in an operating room.

"It's all anecdotal," Sabom concedes, "so you can't consider it proof. But when you get enough of these cases together, you have to wonder if something is going on."

Even a few critics admit to being stumped by such reports.

Yet the evidence for near-death paranormal powers remains shaky at best. Two studies have found that patients' "out-of-body" accounts of what happened in the operating room were wrong. So were the 1988 Armageddon forecasts hyped by Ring and others.

A few hospitals have placed signs in their cardiac units—with nonsensical messages visible only from above—but so far nobody has returned from death claiming to have floated up and seen one.

DIFFERING ACCOUNTS OF NEAR-DEATH EXPERIENCES

Even if some NDEs produce spiritual experiences, that does not resolve the problem of conflicting testimonies. Some people come back believing in reincarnation, some don't; some near-death experiencers do not claim to experience God but only a light; some speak of bliss; some speak of a hellish NDE during which they experienced a sense of darkness and torment and the presence of evil beings intent upon drawing them into doom.

Douglas Groothuis, *Christianity Today*, April 3, 1995.

Some say they discover psychic abilities *after* a near-death trip. Barbara Harris of the International Assn. for Near-Death Studies writes: "My bio-energy field . . . affects electronic equipment. Car batteries are sometimes drained when I'm around . . . street lamps blow out as I walk past."

So widespread are such reports among afterlife veterans (and, notably, among alleged UFO abductees) that when the group proposed its first conference in 1981, some feared the collective psychic energy would spark an electrical and emotional meltdown. Speculation ran rampant, recalls president Nancy Evans Bush: "Perhaps we should have backup generators in case the lights blew, or spiritual emergency trauma teams for emotional storms. Perhaps the entire room would vibrate."

Ten conferences later, nothing extraordinary had happened.

"Where's the documentation?" asks Richard Abanes of Rancho Santa Margarita, California, a Christian researcher and author of *Embraced by the Light and the Bible*. "There's a lot of stories about people who supposedly have psychic powers after their experience, but no one has ever taken them into a laboratory setting to test it."

Which brings us back to Dannion Brinkley. His 1994 book claims that the beings of light in his near-death journey correctly foretold dozens of world events, including the 1991 Persian Gulf War and the 1986 radiation leak at Chernobyl. Unfortunately, as noted by the *Sunday Times of London*, visions of the future are "traditionally revealed before they happen rather than afterwards, thereby making them more convincing."

Still to come, says Brinkley: a 1995 nuclear disaster in Norway and a U.S. economic collapse by 2000.

LIVE NEAR-DEATH EXPERIENCES

One of the most intriguing discoveries about near-death experiences is that people don't have to be "dead" to have them.

Morse writes of two miners who thought they talked with deceased relatives and saw heavenly realms while trapped underground for a few days. Otherworldly visions also turn up in studies of mountaineers who survive falls, prisoners of war and people held hostage by bank robbers, says Dr. Ronald K. Siegel, a professor of psychiatry and bio-behavioral sciences at UCLA.

"The tunnel, the light, the feelings of floating or flying . . . they're all very common," Siegel says. The trigger seems to be "some form of sensory isolation and life-threatening stress."

Scientists call it the *fear*-death experience, says Abanes: "I had one myself in 1980." While being robbed at knifepoint and beaten, "it was like I could see what was happening from outside my body. . . . My whole life flashed before me."

In other instances, fear has nothing to do with it. The *Houston Chronicle* ran an entire article on people who have near-death visions for no apparent reason. One man was "walking out of my greenhouse after tending some plants [when] all of a sudden . . . I was out of my body and on the other side of the room."

He and others in the article apparently saw the same light and felt the same euphoria and sense of mystical knowledge as reported by people who technically died. Indeed, a 1985 survey of International Assn. of Near-Death Studies archives found that only 10% of the visions had any connection to actual "clinical" death.

THE EFFECTS OF DRUGS AND BRAIN STIMULATION

Drugs—including LSD, hashish and the anesthetic Ketamine— also can induce near-death-type sensations, Siegel says.

So can electrical stimulation of the brain. Sixty years ago, Dr.

Wilder Penfield, a neurosurgeon, poked around the right temporal lobe of some epileptic patients and discovered that they would hear heavenly music, relive their pasts in 3-D and have out-of-body visions. Similar experiments continue.

Morse suggests that the right temporal lobe—which he calls "the God sensor of the brain"—is the source of near-death experiences.

Siegel adds: "The [visions are] very concrete, very vivid . . . [and] very powerful . . . [but they're] happening in mental space, not physical space."

Not surprisingly, those who say they have visited the Other Side bristle at suggestions it was illusory. "Realer than real" is how they typically describe the event.

Siegel, however, says near-death experiencers are "mistaking the vividness for truthfulness. . . . They're not aware that hallucinations can occur in a sober, waking state of mind."

But others argue that laboratory-induced hallucinations and afterlife visions are a breed apart. Also, they say, the hallucination theory fails to account for the overnight personality changes that occur, including greater zest for life, improved self-confidence, healthier eating habits and increased compassion.

Adds Morse: "These people aren't just *saying* they're different. They really are. We've documented it beyond a shadow of a doubt. If they said they give more to charities, we checked their tax returns."

That still doesn't prove anything, replies Siegel: "A lot of people who've taken LSD feel changed too. [So do] people who've fallen in love for the first time . . . or people who've been to Vietnam. . . . These are powerful emotional experiences and they change the way we see the world."

Do Experiencers Really Change?

Well, sometimes.

Although near-death testimonials are full of proclamations that the experience reduces their desire for wealth and success, it doesn't seem to stop them from trying to cash in on the light.

Brinkley's manager, Melanie Hill, notes that several afterlife authors charge $7,000 to $10,000 an appearance on the lecture circuit. She calls such fees distasteful, but her own client isn't exactly a pauper. Brinkley clears $1,500 to $2,000 a pop on a schedule of one or two talks a week, she says (although he says many are freebies and that his annual income is just $18,000 to $25,000).

Embraced by the Light author Betty J. Eadie, meanwhile, has incorporated herself. The former hypnotherapist's empire includes a free newsletter, an "Embraced by the Light: The Musical Journey" CD, and a charitable foundation set up to benefit Native Americans, says her assistant. Movie rights are still being negotiated.

Small wonder the field is getting increasingly competitive.

Brinkley upstaged Eadie by "having died not merely once but twice," notes the *National Review*. "And now we have *Beyond the Light* by Phyllis Atwater, who has trumped Mr. Brinkley with a third trip to higher realms."

Even the dust-jacket blurb writers have run out of superlatives. Moody declared Eadie's story "the most profound and complete near-death experience." His praise for Brinkley: "the most amazing and complete near-death experience."

Amazing is an apt description.

Eadie, in addition to saying she revived from death after four hours—nothing short of medically miraculous—also asserts that when Jesus told her that she had to return to this life, she "made [him and the angels] promise that the moment my mission was complete they would take me back [to heaven]. . . . They agreed to my terms." The *National Review* snickers at "this image of Mrs. Eadie negotiating the terms of her departure, with Jesus finally caving in to her demands."

Even the most sincere stories may not be airtight, Morse says. He has tracked a number of them outside the operating room and noticed that details change over time. Part of the problem, he says, is that Moody and most other investigators—by their own admission—ask leading questions in search of evidence to bolster what Morse calls their "New Age . . . political and spiritual agenda."

All of the research should be thrown out and redone, he says.

Until then, Morse basically sides with the skeptics. Sabom, however, offers a compromise stance: He thinks the visions are indeed some kind of foray to spiritual realms, but rejects the idea that they provide glimpses of heaven or hell.

That is a mystery that can never be settled, he says, because the only humans who really know what happens aren't coming back: "We can only resuscitate people, not resurrect them."

| "Past-lives therapy is quick, vivid, relatively inexpensive, and people get better!"

PAST-LIFE MEMORIES CAN BENEFIT PEOPLE

Brian Weiss, interviewed by Nina L. Diamond

Some believers in reincarnation contend that under hypnosis people can remember events from past lives. In the following viewpoint, Brian Weiss, a Miami-based psychiatrist and psychotherapist interviewed by Nina L. Diamond for *Omni* magazine, argues that traumatic events from past lives can cause emotional and physical pain in people's present lives. He maintains that recalling these past-life traumas, through hypnosis if necessary, can help people to overcome present phobias and psychological problems. Weiss is the author of *Many Lives, Many Masters*, which details the past-life therapy of a patient called "Catherine."

As you read, consider the following questions:

1. According to Weiss, what do his patients tell him is the goal of reincarnation?
2. What example does the author give of a physical symptom in the present that may reveal emotional wounds from a past life?
3. In the author's opinion, what are some common misconceptions about hypnosis?

From "Interview: Dr. Brian Weiss," *Omni*, April 1994. Reprinted by permission of *Omni*, ©1994, Omni Publications International, Ltd.

Nina L. Diamond: *Why do scientists find reincarnation a hard concept to buy?*
Weiss: Fear of the unfamiliar. Actually, people don't have to be afraid, if only they'd keep an open mind. Meditation can teach people to do that if they can let go of their fears.

But that can mean changing one's whole life.

Yes, it's scary—but totally safe. It's difficult to let go of the familiar, even if it's harmful, restricting, and blinding.

A History of Reincarnation Beliefs

Where did the concept of reincarnation come from?

It's so far back that we really don't know. I suspect it's from the same place as now: People who are psychic, having visions of it, dreams or déjà vu, memories, meditations, came upon this knowledge. Plato wrote about reincarnation. Ancient civilizations believed in this. We lost this belief only recently, mostly for political reasons. In Judaism, belief in reincarnation, or *gilgul*, existed until the early 1800s. Only with the migration out of Eastern Europe to the West and the need to be accepted in the age of enlightenment and science did the belief go underground—but not in Chasidic [ultraorthodox] populations.

In Christianity, it went underground much earlier—the Second Council of Constantinople in the sixth century declared reincarnation a heresy. Christianity was becoming a state religion, and Romans felt that without the whip of Judgment Day, people would not behave, would not follow. They'd think, "Well, I'll do it next time around."

How do you think the length of time between lifetimes is determined?

People who die violently, or children who die, often return much faster. For those who live longer and die more peacefully, there can be a longer time between lives, 100 years or more.

How many past lives do people generally have?

That varies, but the number that comes up most often in my work is 100, not the thousands and thousands that the Buddhists talk about. . . .

Might two souls meet again in new lives? And if so, how would they recognize each other?

An energy attracts—you're pulled into a situation where you need to be. Perhaps even from the time of birth, in choosing one's parents. It's not random; you choose because of the opportunity to learn. You may make mistakes. Everybody has free will, even your patients. They may not turn out the way you had envisioned, because they have the free will to not reach their potential. In one workshop as we were talking about this, a mother in the audience said to her daughter, "See, you chose me, so stop blaming me!" And the daughter turned to her and said, "Then I must have been in a hurry."

I see love or hostility at first sight as a kind of recognition of souls, a working out of debts and responsibility. Spirit seems thicker than water. That's what really pulls us together—sometimes genetically, but sometimes not. You may be best friends. You may be father and son in one lifetime but lovers in this lifetime. Switching of sex seems frequent. You may have a preference, but you've tried out the other to see what it's like. That's also true of races and religions.

How do you explain souls that in the next lifetime occupy bodies that are biologically damaged?

If it is all to learn—as my patients tell me over and over again—to grow, to become more and more godlike, then whatever the experience, it is a learning experience. Sometimes, though, it's a teaching experience as well, so you may come back into this for others, maybe as an act of charity.

CONSCIOUS MEMORIES OF PAST LIVES

Why don't we consciously remember our past lives?

More and more people are remembering through therapeutic techniques such as hypnosis, but also through dreams, meditation, déjà vu, and when they're in a place they've never been before and they just know their way around. I don't know why we don't all remember. The Greeks believed that when you were born again, you drank from the river of Lethe so you'd forget previous lives.

If we retained knowledge of past lives, would it be cheating, like taking a test with the book open? Are we supposed to learn in each life without benefit from our previous lessons?

Yes. Suppose that between lifetimes you say, "Yeah, I've spent ten lifetimes learning about charity. I know all about it. I'm a charitable person." Okay, now comes the field test. You're born, put into a situation. Is charity ingrained so deeply that you don't have to act charitably because of a specific memory or because it's part of your nature?

So you think we're born with certain values and ideals?

Yes, it gets ingrained, not at the level of the brain, but of the heart, the soul. That's where real learning takes place so that you're not dependent just on what your parents teach you. If one's parents were bigots, for the child to overcome that and become compassionate, understanding, charitable, unbigoted, requires a degree of independence that transcends what we're taught. This is the soul memory in addition to specific talents, abilities, or whatever else the soul might bring back with it. Our real lesson here is to learn of love in all its ramifications—truth, compassion, generosity, mercy.

Past-Life Therapy and Psychoanalysis

The principle of past-life therapy by which basic changes are implemented is similar to that of psychoanalysis—to make the unconscious conscious in order to restore choice. However, in psychoanalysis one seeks the source of an existing condition in some previous trauma or other experience in this lifetime; in past-life therapy it is assumed that the source could be in one or more previous lives. Viewing a *sequence* of lifetimes can sometimes bring about an enhanced understanding of problems, facilitating their alleviation, and it augments self-acceptance through an expansion of awareness.

Willis Harman, *Noetic Sciences Review*, Spring 1994.

Religions and philosophies say the goal is perfection, to become "one with God," the creator or higher being.

That's part of it. But it's like asking a third grader, "What are you learning in arithmetic?" And he says, "I'm learning about addition, long division, and multiplication tables." He can't even comprehend geometry, advanced algebra, and calculus. We're limited by what we know. I suspect the reward has to do with love, merging with higher consciousness, but it may be so far beyond what we can comprehend now; it's hard to put into words. You can sense it when you're on target. You do something compassionate and a tear of joy comes to your eyes.

The Hindus include animals in reincarnation. Have you seen that phenomenon in patients?

I haven't found that myself in doing this work.

Proof of Reincarnation

How can reincarnation be validated with data to support the claims of past lives?

Dr. Ian Stevenson [chairman emeritus of the Department of Psychiatry at the University of Virginia] has more than 2,000 cases of children from all over the world, many of whom exhibit *xenoglossy*, the ability to speak a foreign language to which one has had no exposure. Others know details about places they've never seen. No single individual by his or her story is going to prove reincarnation, but it's the weight of evidence: hundreds of therapists with thousands of patients where this happens—children, nonbelievers, skeptics, all who come out with these details of past lives.

It's very difficult to prove reincarnation scientifically because of what we consider scientific. As a psychiatrist, I'm vitally interested in my patients' clinical improvement. There's no question in my mind or those of the physicians and psychotherapists who are writing and calling me that this has a tremendous therapeutic effect. Past-lives therapy is quick, vivid, relatively inexpensive, and people get better! Right now I'm accumulating evidence that this therapy works and that people, whether they believe in reincarnation or not, can recall details they didn't know from the distant or recent past.

How do past-life relationships affect one's present life?

In every way. Many of your most meaningful relationships are not new. Past lives also affect us in symptoms, emotional and physical. Certain fears and anxieties carry over from other lifetimes. Physical symptoms, where one may have been wounded or hurt in a previous life, frequently come up. In about a dozen obese patients, I've found two patterns that frequently emerge: A person once died emaciated or there was sexual abuse from a past life. A woman decides, "I will never be attractive to men again," and keeps the weight on in this life as a form of protection.

HYPNOSIS AND PAST-LIFE MEMORY

Sometimes people who've never given reincarnation a thought will, under hypnosis during therapy, tap into a past life.

Yes, and frequently that's how therapists, physicians, psychologists, and others have themselves accidentally discovered the field. These memories don't seem to come from an altered state. Many children, when they get a little drowsy at bedtime, when the normal filters are relaxed, come out with details of another time and place. Adults, too, in the hypnagogic state uncover memories. Sometimes a dream may yield a memory fragment—and not a Freudian distortion or wish, symbol, or metaphor.

Often while reliving a past life under hypnosis, patients have technical or detailed knowledge about something they know nothing about in this life. One of the best cases is New Jersey physician Dr. Bob Jarmon's first. It was when he didn't believe in past lives. A Jewish woman in her thirties was seeing him for hypnotherapy for weight loss, and she started developing another symptom: Her periods stopped, and she developed lower abdominal tenderness. She was becoming more anxious, and Jarmon thought she might be pregnant in the Fallopian tube, which can be dangerous because it can burst. When he referred her to a gynecologist, there was no evidence of pregnancy.

She continued to see Jarmon, and they were working on her anxiety when he said, "Go back to the time from which your symptoms first arose." She went back to the Middle Ages and was five months pregnant with an ectopic pregnancy. In that past life, she was Catholic and was with a priest who wouldn't allow abortion or surgery, so she died. And just before she died, she repeated the Catholic act of contrition to the priest, word for word. Jarmon is Catholic and recognized it. The woman had never heard of it.

This happens all the time. I hear details of dress, culture, how to make butter, cheeses, put on roofs, herd goats. But again, it's hard to prove. I've found talents, too, carried over from a past life. I found a young boy who knew the specifications of World War II bombers —he just knew it, because, he said, he flew them when he was big. Children often say that—"Don't you remember when I was big?"

PAST-LIFE MEMORIES AS THERAPY

Give us an example of a dramatic turnaround.

A woman couldn't button the top button of her blouse. By recalling a past life under hypnosis, she learned she'd been guillotined. This had affected her present life's relationships, the ability to trust. Once she remembered the guillotine incident, she was able to close the top button right away, and that set off a chain reaction. It all began to clear up.

But a past life is not necessary for everyone to remember. The subconscious directs the traffic. If it's important and will help you to get rid of a symptom, of course, remembering is necessary, but if it's not, you may not remember the past life. You may remember 5 of your 80 or 90 past lives because only those relate to what you're working on in this life.

How does experiencing a past life affect a person's brain waves?

In hypnosis, you find relaxed alpha and theta brain rhythms. But in past lives, you find all different brain patterns—alpha, beta, theta, visual waves—because the occipital cortex, controlling vision, is stimulated. Using enhanced EEG, I've seen a whole smorgasbord of brain-wave patterns.

What are some misconceptions about reincarnation?

Probably the most famous is that everyone was Napoleon or Julius Caesar. Most of us have been living pretty ordinary lives. There have been even more misconceptions about hypnosis— that it's the only way to have reincarnation memories. Hypnosis is only a state of focused concentration. You're not sleeping; it's not a dream. Your mind is still there; you know where you are.

You don't get stuck in a past life or under hypnosis. You don't have heart attacks; you don't actually reexperience the physical pain or disabilities. You're aware of it but can float above it or stop it at any time.

Have any patients taken a turn for the worse as a result of this therapy?

I still haven't found one. This has to do with the wisdom of the subconscious mind. It will not let something out that harms a person.

REMEMBERING FUTURE LIVES?

Can we go on to future lives?

People are doing this work, such as psychologist Chet Snow, president of the APRT [Association of Past Life Research and Therapy] society. I haven't found it, probably because I'm not looking for it. Mostly I'm doing therapy, and it seems to have some residue from the past. In this lifetime, we look back. At another level, as physicists tell us, there is no time. I tried going into the future with Catherine [Weiss's first past-life patient] right off the bat, and she said it wasn't allowed. You can learn from the past, but the future, that's a series of probabilities. Parallel lives or universes, too, represent alternatives. But to me it's like climbing a tree: The higher up you get, the more committed you are to a particular branch. You're not on the other branches, but they're still there. . . .

Is past-life therapy the next great leap for psychiatry?

Some marvelous breakthroughs will come with the biological understanding of the brain, with understanding Alzheimer's, other memory disorders, schizophrenia, manic-depressive illness. Past-life therapy is also extremely important, and while it may not be the next great leap, it may be the most important.

"The available evidence . . . suggests . . . that 'memories' of having lived a past life are fantasy constructions."

PAST-LIFE MEMORIES ARE FABRICATED

Nicholas P. Spanos, Cheryl A. Burgess, and Melissa Faith Burgess

Research on human memory suggests that people do not recall past events exactly but rather reconstruct them to fit current beliefs and expectations. In the following viewpoint, Nicholas P. Spanos, Cheryl A. Burgess, and Melissa Faith Burgess argue that so-called past-life memories are constructed in much the same way. Believers in reincarnation fantasize past-life memories in order to legitimate their beliefs, the authors assert. Often, Spanos and his colleagues maintain, therapists who believe in reincarnation prompt people under hypnosis to construct these fantasies. The late Nicholas P. Spanos was a professor of psychology at Carleton University in Ottawa, Ontario, Canada. Cheryl A. Burgess is a professor of psychology at the University of Connecticut, Storrs. Melissa Faith Burgess is a research associate at the University of Ottawa Heart Institute.

As you read, consider the following questions:

1. How did Spanos, Menary, and their colleagues, cited by the authors, demonstrate the social nature of past-life identities?
2. What sources do people draw on to flesh out details of their past-life identities, according to the authors?

From Nicholas P. Spanos, Cheryl A. Burgess, and Melissa Faith Burgess, "Past-Life Identities, UFO Abductions, and Satanic Ritual Abuse: The Social Construction of Memories," *International Journal of Clinical and Experimental Hypnosis*, vol. 42, no. 4, pp. 433-46 (October 1994). Published by Sage Publications. Copyright 1994, International Journal of Clinical and Experimental Hypnosis. Reprinted by permission.

It is now generally acknowledged that recall involves reconstructive processes and is strongly influenced by current beliefs and expectations. As pointed out by Frederic C. Bartlett,
author of Remembering, people typically organize their recall of
past events in a way that makes sense of their present situation
and is congruent with their current expectations. What they recall frequently involves a mixture of correctly remembered and
misremembered information that is often impossible to disen-
tangle. Often there is little or no correlation between the accuracy of recall and the confidence that people place in their recall. It is not unusual for people to be convinced about the
accuracy of a remembrance that turns out to be false. Contrary
to popular belief, hypnotic procedures do not reliably enhance
the accuracy of recall and, at least under some circumstances,
may lead subjects to become even more overconfident than
usual in their inaccurate recall. Leading questions and other sug-
gestive interview procedures, whether or not they are administered in a hypnotic context, can produce a very substantial deterioration in recall accuracy even when subjects remain highly
confident in their inaccurate remembrances.

HYPNOSIS AND MEMORY

To a large extent, these ideas about memory have been developed and refined in the context of studying eyewitness testimony. The implications of these ideas have been particularly
influential at shaping the critical attitudes taken by many psychologists toward the reliability of eyewitness testimony, and toward the usefulness of hypnotic and other procedures that are
touted as "refreshing" such testimony. In the typical eyewitness
situation, however, the memory distortions under consideration
involve inaccuracies in detail (e.g., identifying the wrong suspect of a real crime) rather than fabrications of entire complex
scenarios (e.g., detailed descriptions of an entire gun battle that
never occurred). Little systematic research is available that examines the applications of reconstructive and expectancy-guided
views of memory to situations in which people "remember"
entire scenarios that never happened. This article describes research of this kind conducted in our laboratory and examines
the implications of our findings for . . . phenomena that appear
to involve the wholesale "remembering" of fictitious events:
past-life identities.

Several studies have examined factors that influence the formation of false memories by employing the phenomenon of
past-life hypnotic regression. Some believers in reincarnation

contend that people can be hypnotically regressed back to a time before their birth when they led previous lives. The available evidence does not support this hypothesis and suggests instead that "memories" of having lived a past life are fantasy constructions. These fantasy constructions are important, however, because they can shed light on the processes by which people come to treat their fantasies as real, and because past-life identities are similar in many respects to the secondary or alter identities of multiple personality disorder patients. Like multiple personality disorder patients, subjects who report past lives behave as if they are inhabited by secondary selves. These selves display moods and personality characteristics that are different from the person's primary self, have a different name than the primary self, and report memories of which the primary self was previously unaware. Just as multiple personality disorder patients come to believe that their alter identities are real personalities rather than self-generated fantasies, many of the subjects who remember past lives continue to believe in the reality of their past lives after termination of the hypnotic session.

Reima Kampman found that 41% of highly hypnotizable subjects reported a past-life identity and called themselves by different names when given hypnotic suggestions to regress back before their birth. Contrary to the notion that multiple identity experiences are a sign of mental illness, Kampman's past-life responders scored higher on measures of psychological health than did subjects who failed to report a past life.

EXPERIMENTAL CREATION OF PAST-LIFE MEMORIES

In a series of experiments, Nicholas P. Spanos, Evelyn Menary, Natalie J. Gabora, S.C. DuBreuil, and B. Dewhirst also obtained past-life identity reports following hypnotic regression suggestions. Frequently the past-life identities were quite elaborate. They had their own names and frequently described their lives in great detail. Subjects who reported past-life experiences scored higher on measures of hypnotizability and fantasy proneness, but no higher on measures of psychopathology than those who did not exhibit a past life.

The social nature of past-life identities was demonstrated by showing that the characteristics that subjects attributed to these identities were influenced by expectations transmitted by the experimenter. Subjects provided with prehypnotic information about the characteristics of their identities (e.g., information about the identities' expected race and sex) were much more likely than those who did not receive such information to incorporate these characteristics into their descriptions of their past-life selves.

WHY EVERYONE WAS ALWAYS SOMEBODY
IN THEIR PREVIOUS LIFE.

Reprinted by permission of the *Skeptical Inquirer*.

A different study tested the hypothesis that experimenter expectations influence the extent to which past-life identities describe themselves as having been abused during childhood. Before past-life regression, subjects were informed that their past-life identities would be questioned about their childhoods to obtain information about child-rearing practices in earlier historical times. Those in one condition were further told that children in past times had frequently been abused. Those in the other condition were given no information about abuse. The past-life identities of subjects given abuse information reported significantly higher levels of abuse during childhood than did the past-life identities of control subjects. In summary, these studies indicate that both the personal attributes and memory reports elicited from subjects during past-life identity enactments are influenced by the beliefs and expectations conveyed by the experimenter/hypnotist. When constructing their past lives, subjects shape the attributes and biographies attributed to these identities to correspond to their understandings of what significant others believe these characteristics to be.

FACTORS AFFECTING BELIEFS IN PAST LIVES

After termination of the hypnotic regression procedure, some past-life reporters believed that their past-life experiences were memories of actual, reincarnated personalities, whereas others believed that their past-life identities were imaginary creations. Hypnotizability did not predict the extent to which subjects assigned credibility to their past-life identities. Instead, the degree of credibility assigned to these experiences correlated significantly with the degree to which subjects believed in reincarnation before the experiment, and the extent to which they expected to experience a real past life.

In a final study Spanos, Menary, et al. manipulated prehypnotic information that concerned the reality of past-life experiences. Subjects in one condition were informed that past-life experiences were interesting fantasies rather than evidence of real past-life memories. Those in another condition were provided with background information which suggested that reincarnation was a scientifically credible notion, and that past-life identities were real people who had lived earlier lives. Subjects in the two conditions were equally likely to construct past-life experiences, but those assigned to the imaginary creation condition assigned significantly less credibility to these identities than did those told that reincarnation was scientifically credible.

Taken together these findings indicate that experiences of having lived a past life are social creations that can be elicited easily from many normal people, and that are determined by the understandings that subjects develop about such experiences from the information to which they are exposed. Past-life identities can be quite complex and detailed, and subjects draw from a wide array of sources outside of the immediate situation (e.g., television shows, historical novels, aspects of their own past, wish-fulfilling daydreams) to flesh out their newly constructed identity and to provide it with the history and characteristics that are called for by their understanding of the current task demands. The most important factor in influencing the extent to which past-life experiences are defined as real memories appears to be the extent to which subjects hold a belief system that is congruent with this interpretation (i.e., a belief in reincarnation). Information from an authoritative source which legitimates or delegitimates reincarnation beliefs also influences the extent to which subjects define their experiences as real memories rather than imaginings.

All of these past-life experiments either tested only highly hypnotizable subjects or found that the reporting of past lives was correlated significantly with hypnotizability. Hypnotizability refers to the extent to which subjects respond to hypnotic suggestions, and it correlates significantly with such dimensions as fantasy proneness and an openness to unusual experiences. One interpretation suggests that hypnotizability or its imaginal correlates may constitute cognitive abilities which predispose individuals to construct secondary identities when such experiences are called for by contextual demands, and when these subjects are motivated to respond to those demands. However, an alternative hypothesis suggests that hypnotizability is correlated with the development of past-life identities because the suggestions that called for these experiences were administered in a hypnotic context and therefore were likely to call up the same attitudes and expectations as the hypnotizability test situation. Whether circumstances can be created that will elicit multiple identity enactments from low hypnotizables remains to be determined. . . .

PAST-LIFE MEMORIES ARE FANTASIES

The findings reviewed above are consistent with the view that recall is reconstructive and guided by current motivations and expectations. In addition, these findings indicate that social factors can lead people to generate complex fantasy scenarios and to define such experiences as actual memories of real events. In many cases some elements in these fantasies are memories. For instance, past-life reporters frequently incorporate information from their own past, or events and plots recalled from books and movies into their past-life identities. . . . Despite the inclusion of real memory elements, however, past-life, . . ."memories" are primarily fantasy constructions. Typically they are organized around expectations derived from external sources, embedded in a belief system that is congruent with their classification as memories, and legitimated as memories by significant others. In short, whether experiences are counted as memories of actual happenings or as fantasies may, under some circumstances, have less to do with characteristics intrinsic to these experiences than to the internal context (i.e., supportive belief structures) in which they are embedded and the external context (i.e., social legitimation) in which they are validated.

PERIODICAL BIBLIOGRAPHY

The following articles have been selected to supplement the diverse views presented in this chapter. Addresses are provided for periodicals not indexed in the *Readers' Guide to Periodical Literature*, the *Alternative Press Index*, the *Social Sciences Index*, or the *Index to Legal Periodicals and Books*.

Richard Abanes	"Readers Embrace the Light," *Christianity Today*, March 7, 1994.
Betty J. Eadie	"Looking at Life," *Ladies' Home Journal*, January 1995.
Sheila Anne Feeney	"Back from Death: Three Women's Incredible Stories," *McCall's*, December 1994.
Diane Goldner	"Remembrances of Lives Past," *New Age Journal*, November/December 1994. Available from 42 Pleasant St., Watertown, MA 02172.
Douglas Groothuis	"To Heaven and Back?" *Christianity Today*, April 3, 1995.
David Ives	"Night of the Living Near-Dead," *New York Times Magazine*, November 27, 1994.
Tracy Johnston	"Struck by Lightning," *Harper's Bazaar*, June 1994.
John F. Kavanaugh	"After Life," *America*, April 29, 1995.
John F. Kavanaugh	"The Great Union," *America*, November 4, 1995.
Laura Darlene Lansberry	"First-Person Report: A Skeptic's Near-Death Experience," *Skeptical Inquirer*, Summer 1994.
Frederick Levine	"Can 'Past-Life' Therapy Help You in This Lifetime?" *Natural Health*, November/December 1993. Available from 17 Station St., Brookline Village, MA 02147.
James Martin	"Of Many Things," *America*, October 22, 1994.
Terry Mattingly	"Brilliant Orbs and 'God Lite,'" *Moody*, January 1995.
Raymond Moody with Paul Perry	"Through the Looking Glass," *New Age Journal*, November/December 1993.
Jonathan Rosen	"Rewriting the End: Elizabeth Kübler-Ross," *New York Times Magazine*, January 22, 1995.
Richard Selzer	"Raising the Dead," *Discover*, February 1994.

FOR FURTHER DISCUSSION

CHAPTER 1

1. Roger L. Welsch contends that scientists' rejection of the existence of ghosts is based on a folk belief (or superstition) rather than a scientific principle. What position should a scientist take toward unexplained phenomena, in his opinion? In Bryan Farha's view, what stance should scientists take regarding paranormal phenomena? How do you think Farha would respond to Welsch's argument? Defend your answer using examples from the text.

2. William Evans argues that a number of television programs and movies promote belief in the paranormal. Why are such television shows popular, in his view? According to Loyd Auerbach, why is the number of television shows depicting paranormal phenomena increasing? What does he hope people will learn from these television shows?

CHAPTER 2

1. Donald W. Goldsmith and Tobias C. Owen argue that most UFOs can be explained as natural occurrences and therefore scientists should remain skeptical about the existence of alien spacecraft. In Alan Acree's account of a UFO sighting, what possible mundane explanations does he consider? In his view, why should scientists maintain open minds about the possibility of extraterrestrial spacecraft?

2. John E. Mack maintains that a small number of people have been abducted by aliens and subjected to biological examinations and experiments. In his view, what does the similarity in detail between abduction accounts suggest? What other evidence exists to support the veracity of the stories, according to Mack? In Susan Blackmore's opinion, what is suggested by the similarity between contemporary alien abduction accounts and past stories of fairies and demons? In your opinion, which argument is more believable? Explain.

3. Air force officers Richard L. Weaver and James McAndrew, who conducted a thorough search for military records related to UFOs, maintain that the U.S. government is not concealing evidence of the existence of extraterrestrial spaceships. What evidence do the officers present to support their argument that the military was not involved in the recovery of a spaceship in 1947? In Dennis Stacy's opinion, what does the military's reluctance to publish UFO documents requested under

the Freedom of Information Act suggest? What evidence does he present that the air force covered up the crash of a spaceship in 1947? Which evidence do you find more persuasive, and why?

CHAPTER 3

1. Daryl J. Bem maintains that the ganzfeld experiment, which attempts to demonstrate ESP, has been replicated enough times by enough independent researchers to scientifically establish the existence of ESP. What is Susan Blackmore's objection to the ganzfeld experiments conducted by Carl Sargent? Do you agree or disagree with Blackmore that this problem casts doubt on all of the experiments? Support your answer using examples from the text.

2. Harold E. Puthoff relates some anecdotal successes from the CIA's experiments in remote viewing (psychic spying). In Ray Hyman's opinion, why do the results of the CIA's experiments fail to prove the existence of a paranormal phenomenon? What possible alternative explanations for the results of the experiments does Hyman offer? In your opinion, could one of Hyman's alternative explanations account for the results described by Puthoff? Cite examples from the viewpoints to defend your opinion.

3. Mary T. Browne is a psychic who offers what she believes is therapeutic advice to people. In Mark Matousek's opinion, why is the advice of psychics often harmful to people? Do you think that advice from psychics is harmful, harmless, or helpful? Explain your answer using evidence from the viewpoints.

CHAPTER 4

1. Beverly C. Jaegers maintains that the similarity of near-death experiences proves that life after death exists. In Roy Rivenburg's opinion, what is the significance of discrepancies in near-death accounts? According to Rivenburg, what types of experiments have simulated near-death experiences? How does Jaeger counter the evidence of these experiments? Which argument do you find more persuasive, and why?

2. Brian Weiss maintains that people can recall past lives through hypnosis. According to Nicholas P. Spanos, Cheryl A. Burgess, and Melissa Faith Burgess, what do people actually "remember" when under hypnosis? Based on his viewpoint, how do you think Weiss would respond to this argument? Cite the text to support your answer.

ORGANIZATIONS TO CONTACT

The editors have compiled the following list of organizations concerned with the issues debated in this book. The descriptions are derived from materials provided by the organizations. All have publications or information available for interested readers. The list was compiled on the date of publication of the present volume; names, addresses, phone and fax numbers, and e-mail and Internet addresses may change. Be aware that many organizations take several weeks or longer to respond to inquiries, so allow as much time as possible.

The Academy of Religion and Psychical Research
PO Box 614, Bloomfield, CT 06002-0614
(203) 242-4593

The academy focuses specifically on the area where religion and psychic research interface. It views parapsychology as providing the authoritative model of empirical science as well as having a bearing upon religious claims. It publishes the scholarly quarterly *Journal of Religion and Psychical Research* and the quarterly newsletter *ARPR Bulletin*.

Amalgamated Flying Saucer Clubs of America (AFSCA)
PO Box 39, Yucca Valley, CA 92286-0039
(619) 365-1141

AFSCA's goal is to inform the public about the reality of flying saucers and to bring about true world peace in cooperation with beings from other planets and star systems. The club is a major source of "contactee-oriented" flying saucer information, including photographs, contactee reports, and over three hundred titles on the subject of flying saucers. AFSCA publishes the quarterly newsletter *Flying Saucers International* and a variety of information sheets.

American Association for Parapsychology (AAP)
PO Box 225, Canoga Park, CA 91305
(818) 883-0840 • fax: (818) 884-1850

The AAP strives to provide a better understanding of the scientific basis for psychic phenomena and to utilize this knowledge for the betterment of humankind. Through its comprehensive study course on the science of parapsychology, the association attempts to bridge the gap between psychic research in the natural and social sciences with that of research in philosophy and comparative religion. It publishes various outlines and research guides.

American Society for Psychical Research (ASPR)
5 W. 73rd St., New York, NY 10023
(212) 799-5050 • fax: (212) 496-2497

The ASPR seeks to advance the understanding of psychic phenomena. Through its research and educational programs, the society supports the efforts of both laypersons and professionals to use the study of psychic phenomena to expand and improve the understanding of human nature and the broad scope of human abilities. The ASPR publishes the *ASPR Newsletter* and the *Journal of the American Society for Psychical Research*, both quarterly, as well as numerous books and audio and videotapes.

Borderland Sciences Research Foundation
PO Box 220, Bayside, CA 95524
(707) 825-7733 • fax: (707) 825-7799

The foundation is composed of individuals interested in the borderland between visible and invisible reality. It attempts to explore phenomena that orthodox science either cannot or will not investigate. Among the foundation's numerous publications are the books *Extraterrestrial Archaeology: Incredible Proof We Are Not Alone*, *Man-Made UFOs*, and *The Cosmic Pulse of Life: The Revolutionary Biological Power Behind UFOs*.

Center for Bigfoot Studies (CBS)
10926 Milano Ave., Norwalk, CA 90650-1638
(714) 921-1014

CBS seeks to establish the physical reality of Bigfoot, a large, humanlike creature reputedly inhabiting wilderness regions of North America. The center works to obtain the support of interested scientists and other Bigfoot researchers. CBS publishes *Big Footnotes: A Comprehensive Bibliography Concerning Bigfoot, the Abominable Snowmen, and Related Beings* and the booklet *Bigfoot at Bluff Creek*.

Committee for the Scientific Investigation of Claims of the Paranormal (CSICOP)
PO Box 703, Amherst, NY 14226-0703
(716) 636-1425 • fax: (716) 636-1733

CSICOP is a scientific and educational organization composed of individuals interested in studying claims of paranormal phenomena. It encourages critical investigation of paranormal and fringe-science claims from a strictly scientific point of view and disseminates factual information about the results of such inquiries to the scientific community and the public. CSICOP publishes the bimonthly magazine *Skeptical Inquirer*.

Fund for UFO Research
PO Box 277, Mount Rainier, MD 20712
(703) 684-6032 • fax: (703) 684-6032

The fund is the first organization exclusively dedicated to providing financial support for scientific research into all aspects of the UFO phenomenon. A board of directors reviews research proposals on their merits and approves those that show the greatest promise of advancing scientific knowledge and public understanding of UFOs. Numerous publications are available through the fund, including the newsletter Fund for UFO Research: Quarterly Report, the book Project Delta: A Study of Multiple UFO, and the report "UFO Crash/Retrievals: Search for Proof in a Hall of Mirrors."

The J. Allen Hynek Center for UFO Studies (CUFOS)
2457 W. Peterson Ave., Chicago, IL 60659
(312) 271-3611 • fax: (312) 465-1898
CUFOS is an international group of scientists, academics, investigators, and volunteers dedicated to the continuing examination and analysis of the UFO phenomenon. The center acts as a clearinghouse where UFO experiences can be both reported and researched. It publishes the bimonthly magazine International UFO Reporter and the book Encounter at Buff Ledge: A UFO Case History.

Mind Development and Control Association
9633 Cinnabar Dr., Sappington, MO 63126
(314) 849-3722
The association develops and promotes interest in various facets of paranormal and psychic research. It provides monthly correspondence lessons in psychic arts and sciences as well as classes in psychic development and ESP skills. The association publishes the U.S. Psi Squad.

Parapsychology Foundation
228 E. 71st St., New York, NY 10021
(212) 628-1550 • fax: (212) 628-1559
The foundation was established in 1951 to promote and support impartial scientific inquiry into the psychic aspects of human nature. It encourages scientific investigators to pursue independent studies of the human mind, and it acts as a clearinghouse for parapsychological information. The foundation publishes the booklet Guide to Sources of Information on Parapsychology, the reprint of the tribute "Eileen J. Garrett: A Woman Who Made a Difference," and back issues of the foundation's former journal Parapsychology Review.

Rhine Research Center
Institute for Parapsychology
402 N. Buchanan Blvd., Durham, NC 27701-1728
(919) 688-8241 • fax: (919) 683-4338

The center is a research and educational organization established to explore unusual types of experiences that suggest capabilities yet unrecognized in the realm of human personality. It seeks to bridge gaps between the academic community and independent researchers and between the general public and the research laboratory. Among the center's numerous publications are the quarterly *Journal of Parapsychology* and the books *Parapsychology: The Controversial Science, Explaining the Unexplained: Mysteries of the Paranormal,* and *What Survives? Contemporary Explorations of Life After Death.*

SETI League

PO Box 555, Little Ferry, NJ 07643
voice-mail: (201) 641-1770 • fax: (201) 641-1771
e-mail: info@setileague.org • Internet: http://www.setileague.org

The SETI League is a membership-supported, nonprofit educational and scientific organization dedicated to the electromagnetic search for extraterrestrial intelligence. Recognizing that receipt of signals of intelligent origin from beyond Earth will change forever the view of humanity's place in the cosmos, it envisions a worldwide network of thousands of advanced experimenters working together to hasten mankind's entry into the galactic community. Its publications include the books *Project Cyclops,* the *SETI League Technical Manual,* and *Sing a Song of SETI* as well as the quarterly newsletter *SearchLites.*

Skeptics Society

PO Box 338, Altadena, CA 91001
(818) 794-3119 • fax: (818) 794-1301
e-mail: skepticmag@aol.com

The society is composed of scholars, scientists, and historians who promote the use of scientific methods to scrutinize such nonscientific traditions as religion, superstition, mysticism, and New Age beliefs. It is devoted to the investigation of extraordinary claims and revolutionary ideas and to the promotion of science and critical thinking. The society publishes the quarterly *Skeptic Magazine.*

Society for Scientific Exploration (SSE)

PO Box 3818, Charlottesville, VA 22903
fax: (804) 924-3104 • Internet: http://www.jse.com

Affiliated with the University of Virginia's Department of Astronomy, the society seeks to provide a professional forum for presentations, criticisms, and debates concerning topics that are ignored or given inadequate study by mainstream academia. It wants to increase understanding of the factors that at present limit the scope of scientific inquiry. The society publishes the quarterlies *Journal of Scientific Exploration* and *Explorer.* The journal is available from PO Box 5848, Stanford, CA 94309-5848.

Survival Research Foundation (SRF)

PO Box 63-0026, Miami, FL 33163-0026

(305) 936-1408

The SRF searches for valid evidence of postmortem survival and communication. It conducts research on near-death experiences and presents the results to universities and the public through publications and lectures. Among the foundation's publications are the *Encyclopedia of Parapsychology and Psychical Research* and the papers "Death Comes Alive" and "Tests for Communication with the Dead."

UFO Information Retrieval Center (UFOIRC)

3131 W. Cochise Dr., No. 158, Phoenix, AZ 85051-9501

(602) 997-1523 • fax: (602) 870-3178

e-mail: 71303.3615@compuserve.com

The center collects, analyzes, publishes, and disseminates information on reports of unidentified flying objects. It also compiles statistics and sponsors photo exhibits pertaining to UFOs. UFOIRC publishes a bibliography of UFO-related books, periodicals, and videotapes as well as the periodical *Reference for Outstanding UFO Sighting Reports*.

Vampire Information Exchange (VIE)

PO Box 290328, Brooklyn, NY 11229-0328

Founded in 1978, VIE is an organization of individuals interested in vampires. It distributes information on vampires and vampirism in both fact and fiction and publishes the *VIE Newsletter* five to six times a year.

BIBLIOGRAPHY OF BOOKS

Leonard Angel

Enlightenment East and West. Albany: State University of New York Press, 1994.

P.M.H. Atwater

Future Memory: How Those Who See the Future Shed New Light on the Workings of the Human Mind. New York: Carol Publishing, 1996.

Lee W. Bailey and Jenny Yates

The Near-Death Experience: A Reader. New York: Routledge, 1996.

Carl Becker

Paranormal Experience and Survival of Death. Albany: State University of New York Press, 1993.

John Beloff

Parapsychology: A Concise History. New York: St. Martin's, 1993.

Susan Blackmore

Dying to Live: Near Death Experiences. Buffalo, NY: Prometheus, 1993.

Jerome Clark

UFO Encounters and Beyond. New York: Signet, 1993.

Jerome Clark

The UFO Encyclopedia. Detroit: Apogee, 1990–1996.

Harry M. Collins and Trevor Pinch

The Golem: What Everyone Should Know About Science. New York: Cambridge University Press, 1993.

Michael Craft

Alien Impact. New York: St. Martin's, 1996.

David J. Darling

Zen Physics: The Science of Death, the Logic of Reincarnation. New York: HarperCollins, 1996.

Paul Davies

Are We Alone? Philosophical Implications of the Discovery of Extraterrestrial Life. New York: BasicBooks, 1995.

Christian De Duve

Vital Dust: Life as a Cosmic Imperative. New York: BasicBooks, 1995.

Steven J. Dick

The Biological Universe: The Twentieth-Century Extraterrestrial Life Debate and the Limits of Science. New York: Cambridge University Press, 1996.

Betty J. Eadie

Embraced by the Light. Placerville, CA: Gold Leaf Press, 1992.

Paul Edwards

Reincarnation: A Critical Examination. Buffalo, NY: Prometheus, 1996.

Martin Gardner

The Night Is Large. New York: St. Martin's, 1996.

Leonard George

Alternative Realities: The Paranormal, the Mystic, and the Transcendent in Human Experience. New York: Facts On File, 1995.

Donald W. Goldsmith and Tobias C. Owen

The Search for Life in the Universe. 2nd ed. Reading, MA: Addison-Wesley, 1992.

Rosemary Ellen Guiley — *Harper's Encyclopedia of Mystical and Paranormal Experience.* San Francisco: Harper, 1991.

Jean Heidmann — *Extraterrestrial Intelligence.* New York: Cambridge University Press, 1995.

David J. Hess — *Science in the New Age: The Paranormal, Its Defenders and Debunkers, and American Culture.* Madison: University of Wisconsin Press, 1993.

Gerald Holton — *Science and Antiscience.* Cambridge, MA: Harvard University Press, 1993.

Hans Holzer — *Tales at Midnight: True Stories from Parapsychology Casebooks and Journals.* Philadelphia: Courage Books, 1994.

David Michael Jacobs — *Secret Life: Firsthand Accounts of UFO Abductions.* New York: Simon & Schuster, 1992.

Lynn Kear — *Reincarnation: A Selected Annotated Bibliography.* Westport, CT: Greenwood Press, 1996.

Allan Kellehear — *Experiences Near Death: Beyond Medicine and Religion.* New York: Oxford University Press, 1995.

Paul Kurtz — *The New Skepticism: Inquiry and Reliable Knowledge.* Buffalo, NY: Prometheus, 1992.

Paul Kurtz and Timothy J. Madigan — *Challenges to the Enlightenment: In Defense of Reason and Science.* Buffalo, NY: Prometheus, 1994.

Scott Mandelker — *From Elsewhere: Being E.T. in America.* New York: Birch Lane Press, 1995.

Mark Matousek — *Sex, Death, Enlightenment: A True Story.* New York: Riverhead Books, 1996.

Melvin Morse — *Transformed by the Light: The Powerful Effect of Near-Death Experiences on People's Lives.* New York: Villard, 1992.

Joe Nickell — *Entities: Angels, Spirits, Demons, and Other Alien Beings.* Buffalo, NY: Prometheus, 1995.

Joe Nickell — *Psychic Sleuths: ESP and Sensational Cases.* Buffalo, NY: Prometheus, 1994.

Curtis Peebles — *Watch the Skies! A Chronicle of the Flying Saucer Myth.* Washington, DC: Smithsonian Institution Press, 1994.

Kevin Randle — *Roswell UFO Crash Update: Exposing the Military Coverup of the Century.* New Brunswick, NJ: Global Communications, 1996.

Kenneth Ring — *The Omega Project: Near-Death Experiences, UFO Encounters, and Mind at Large.* New York: William Morrow, 1992.

David Ritchie   *UFO:The Definitive Guide to Unidentified Flying Objects and Related Phenomena.* New York: Facts On File, 1994.

Andrew Ross   *Strange Weather: Culture, Science, and Technology in the Age of Limits.* New York: Verso, 1991.

Andrew Ross and   *Technoculture.* Minneapolis: University of
Constance Penley   Minnesota Press, 1991.

Carl Sagan   *The Demon-Haunted World: Science as a Candle in the Dark.* New York: Random House, 1995.

Margaret Singer   *Cults in Our Midst.* San Francisco: Jossey-Bass,
and Janja Lalich   1995.

Gordon Stein   *Encyclopedia of the Paranormal.* Amherst, NY: Prometheus, 1996.

Nancy H. Traill   *Possible Worlds of the Fantastic: The Rise of the Paranormal in Fiction.* Toronto: University of Toronto Press, 1996.

Brian L. Weiss   *Through Time into Healing.* New York: Simon & Schuster, 1993.

Roger L. Welsch   *Touching the Fire: Buffalo Dancers, the Sky Bundle, and Other Tales.* New York: Villard, 1992.

Ben Zuckerman   *Extraterrestrials: Where Are They?* 2nd ed. New York:
and Michael Hart   Cambridge University Press, 1995.

INDEX

as unsuitable for life, 78, 79
Miller-Urey experiment, 70
Moody, Raymond, 161, 166, 168
Morse, Melvin, 167, 170, 171, 172
Murdoch, Rupert, 54
Musser, George, 23

Naeye, Robert, 76
NASA, 106
  Ames Research Center, 71, 72
  and *Pioneer 10* flyby, 134
National Geographic, 140
National Research Council (NRC), 127,
  128, 138, 140
National Review, 172
National Security Agency (NSA), 105,
  106, 132-33
NBC television network, 45, 52, 55
near-death experiences (NDEs), 55
  as hallucinations, 165-72
    are inconsistent, 166-67
    are unreliable predictions of future, 170
    drug-induced, 170-71
  as visions of afterlife, 158-64
    in childhood, 159-60
    common elements of, 160-62
    popular interest in, 55
New Age Journal, 161
Newton, Isaac, 36, 39
New York Times, 115
New York Times Magazine, 88
Nicholson, Richard S., 26, 27
Noetic Sciences Review, 134, 176
North American Aerospace Defense
  Command (NORAD), 104

Oberbeck, Verne, 71
Oberg, James, 107
One Step Beyond (television series), 51
Osis, Karlis, 167
Overbye, Dennis, 26
Owen, Tobias C., 65

Palmer, John, 142
Paque, Julie, 68
Paramount Domestic Television, 55, 56
paranormal phenomena
  may be related to brain function, 93
  and need for logic/research, 17-20
  and need for open mind, 21-24, 34-41
    because anomalies arise, 35
    because curiosity leads to discovery, 39
    because new discoveries may be
      repressed, 37-39
  popular acceptance of, 27-33
    and ignorance/superstition, 26-33
    is increasing, 27
  see also ESP; near-death experiences;

parapsychology; psychics; television
  shows
parapsychology, 36, 38, 41
  increased support for, 27
  media representation of, 51
past-life memories, 146-47
  benefits of, 173, 176, 177-79
  fabrication of, 180-85
    and expectations of researchers, 183-84
    under hypnotic suggestion, 181-82
  see also reincarnation
Pauling, Linda and Linus, 39
Peebles, Curtis, 102
Penfield, Wilder, 171
Persinger, Michael, 93
Planetary Report, 79
Poese, Earl, 163
Poltergeist III (movie), 45-46, 47
Presley, Elvis, sightings, 166, 168
Price, Pat, 135
Pritchard, David, 88
Proctor, Timothy, 101
Project on Government and Secrecy, 106
psychic phenomena (psi). *See* ESP; near-
  death experiences; paranormal
  phenomena; psychics
psychics
  do not relate bad news, 153
  harm people, 149-54
    through irresponsibility, 152
  help people, 144-48
  and religious community, 147-48
Psychological Bulletin, 123, 124, 127, 129,
  138
Psychology Today, 144
Puthoff, Harold E., 131, 138, 139

Rae, Stephen, 88
Ramey, Roger, 101, 102, 111, 112
Randle, Kevin, 113
Raso, Peggy, 160, 161, 162
reincarnation, 53, 173
  history of, 174-75
  misunderstanding of, 178-79
  proof of, 176-77
  see also past-life memories
ReVision, 38
Rhine, Joseph Banks, 122
Ring, Kenneth, 161, 165, 167, 168, 169
Rivenburg, Roy, 165
RNA, 69, 70
Rosenthal, Robert, 127
Roswell Daily Record, 101, 111
Roswell incident. *See under* UFOs

Sabom, Michael, 168, 169
Sagan, Carl, 28, 40, 49, 96
Salina, Kansas, 18, 19